THE SPORTING SHOOTER'S HANDBOOK

THE SPORTING SHOOTER'S HANDBOOK

An introduction to the sport

GRAHAM DOWNING

Quiller

Based on previous publication *Shooting for Beginners* 1996, 2nd Edition 2003

First published in the UK in 2018
by Quiller, an imprint of Quiller Publishing Ltd

British Library Cataloguing-in-Publication Data
A catalogue record for this book is available from the British Library

ISBN 978 1 84689 260 8

Gender disclaimer: the use of the word 'his' implies 'hers'.

Internal design and layout by Arabella Ainslie

Printed in China

Quiller
An imprint of Quiller Publishing Ltd
Wykey House, Wykey, Shrewsbury, SY4 1JA
Tel: 01939 261616
Email: info@quillerbooks.com
www.quillerpublishing.com

CONTENTS

Introduction

INTRODUCTION

SHOOTING is a popular participant sport, a force for conservation and an important part of the rural economy. In Britain at least 600,000 people go shooting, and while a third of them shoot targets or clay pigeons, the remainder go out into the countryside to hunt live quarry, whether for sport or to control pests. In doing so they are following a tradition that traces its roots back hundreds of years, one that has played a major part in the creation of the landscape we see today.

Sporting shooting provides pleasure and satisfaction in a number of different ways. For the vast majority of us who live in towns and cities, it provides the opportunity to get out into the countryside, to enjoy the surroundings of fields, woods, moors and marshes and to exercise those hunting skills and instincts that are deep within all of us. In doing so we learn to appreciate and respect the countryside, its

Shooting provides the opportunity to get out into the countryside.

traditions and its way of life, while participating in an activity that is so absorbing that it has the capacity to take our minds completely off the worries off the everyday world.

Some branches of the sport, like game shooting, involve meeting and mixing with other people, and the friendships that are formed and the companionship that develops in the shooting field is enjoyed and appreciated by many. Other shooters pursue more solitary forms of the sport. The wildfowler on the lonely marshes at dawn or the pigeon shooter in his hide derive their pleasure from the challenge that comes from pitting their own wits against those of a truly wild quarry. They know that only when their hunting skills are honed to perfection are they likely to achieve success and come home with ducks, geese or woodpigeons in their game bags.

Yet, others are absorbed by the relationship between the shooter and their age-old hunting companion, the working dog. Handling, training and breeding gundogs requires endless patience and dedication, but the pleasure and satisfaction to be gained from forging a partnership with a working gundog is enormous. For many shooters, working their dog is a central part of the attraction of shooting, and indeed there are plenty who are quite happy to leave the gun at home and instead enjoy a day's beating with their spaniel or picking-up with their retriever.

A further pleasure that shooting provides is that which is enjoyed around the dinner table, for with the exception of a very few birds or animals that are shot purely for the purposes of pest control, everything that the shooter brings home in his game bag provides wholesome and delicious food. There has been an explosion of interest in wild meat such as game and venison among Britain's TV and celebrity chefs, and the UK game market has grown strongly as a result. It is not surprising that game, venison and other wild food from the countryside is increasingly sought after by those who are looking for a more natural, healthy way of eating.

Game birds, pigeons, wildfowl, rabbits and hares are low in fat and, because they have all fed on a rich and varied diet from the fields, woods and hedgerows, they are full of flavour.

Shooting provides valuable income to the economy. Each year, shooters spend around £2.5 billion on goods and services by buying guns, ammunition, clothing and accessories; on travel and

There are many opportunities open to young shooters.

accommodation, and on fees to the sporting estates, syndicates and clubs which provide shooting opportunities. These fees pay for the cost of game birds, cover crops and habitat management, plus of course the wages of gamekeepers and other shoot helpers. Because most shoots buy services and employ staff from within a radius of 10 to 15 miles, this means that large amounts of money are brought into rural areas. The importance of this income for small rural businesses such as pubs and hotels, much of it coming during the autumn and winter months when revenue from tourism is at its lowest, is very significant, especially in remote areas such as the north Pennines and the Scottish highlands. Shooting supports around 74,000 jobs, about half of which are those of the gamekeepers, beaters and shoot managers employed by the estates that provide shooting opportunity. The remainder are those supported by downstream businesses such as the 2,000 gun shops and trade outlets that employ up to 10,000 people and sell goods worth £200–£300 million a year, including 170 million cartridges. Shooting also ensures the maintenance of the British gun trade with its long tradition of manufacturing very high-quality sporting firearms.

Along with its value to the wider economy, shooting provides important benefits to the wellbeing of its participants and those involved in its associated activities such as picking-up and beating. It improves people's happiness and adds to their enjoyment of life, providing escape from the stresses of daily routine. The physical activity involved in a day's shooting is valuable in promoting and maintaining fitness, while the outdoor nature of the sport enables participants to engage with the natural environment. A recent survey by the British Association for Shooting and Conservation (BASC) showed that shooting was important to the personal wellbeing of the overwhelming majority of respondents, and over half said that the feeling of wellbeing that shooting gave them was a reason for taking part. Shooting also enables its participants to meet people from all walks of life and to spend time and socialise with them, often promoting lifelong friendships. It is not too far fetched to suggest that in some rural areas it is part of the cement that helps bind the community together.

Shooting is a valuable contributor to personal wellbeing.

Where farmers and landowners have been interested in shooting, they have always created an attractive and diverse landscape with woods, hedgerows and wetlands that are favoured by game birds and animals. Country estates were very often laid out for shooting. Their landscapes, which are today admired and cherished, are still maintained in the traditional manner because of the sport that they provide. But the value of shooting to the conservation of landscapes and wildlife results not merely from what has been done in the past: the farms and estates that provide shooting today spend around £250 million annually on conservation work, more than eight times the amount spent by the RSPB on

As well as helping to maintain communities, shooting also preserves the landscape and its wildlife.

conservation on its reserves in 2013. Sporting farmers and landowners are well aware of the importance to game birds of small woods and spinneys, hedgerows, ponds, streams and diverse field margins that are rich in insect life. It therefore comes as no surprise that they are amongst the most active participants in environmental schemes such as Countryside Stewardship, so where shooting takes place, more land is brought into conservation management.

It is not just pheasants and partridges that benefit from the countryside management that is undertaken in the name of shooting. Wildlife of all sorts thrives in the rich and secure habitats that are created, from wild birds and mammals to butterflies and rare plants. This fact is well recognised by all of the leading conservation agencies and voluntary bodies, which in turn rely on shooting groups such as wildfowling clubs to help warden and protect their own wildlife reserves.

There remains, however, the dilemma in many people's minds that while shooting may well conserve some birds and animals, it directly causes the death of others. One cannot escape the fact that if you are planning to go shooting, then the consequence may well be that a pheasant, rabbit or duck is killed. It is therefore argued by some that shooters damage wildlife, and that they must be cruel and barbaric.

Where shooting occurs, more land is brought into conservation management.

In fact, shooters preserve far more wildlife than they destroy. While every hunter will go to great lengths to seek to kill his quarry, his aim is only to harvest the natural increment that every quarry species produces each year. The shooter will always want to ensure that there is plenty left to breed and reproduce in order that there may continue to be birds and animals to hunt in the future. This is known as the principle of 'wise use' of game.

While commercial hunters have been responsible for the wiping out of entire species, sporting shooters have been at pains to ensure that, although an individual animal may die in the course of the hunt, the species as a whole will survive and flourish. The crucial difference between the commercial hunter and the sporting shooter is that while the one derives economic benefit from the dead creature, whether from its hide, meat or other commodities, the other derives his 'benefit' or enjoyment and satisfaction from the hunt itself. Often, he sets self-imposed conditions that deliberately make it harder for him to kill his quarry. To the commercial hunter, returning empty-handed from a hunting trip represents economic loss; the true sporting shooter, on the other hand, accepts a blank day with equanimity. The shooter is enriched as much by an 'unsuccessful' hunting trip as by one that results in a full game bag.

Since the earliest times hunters have protected the creatures they pursue by imposing close seasons during the breeding period, and by restricting the ways in which birds or animals may be killed or taken. Such regulation has often distinguished sporting shooting from commercial hunting.

The charge of cruelty is often made by those who describe shooting as a 'bloodsport'. However, no shooter ever deliberately seeks to inflict cruelty, that is to say unnecessary suffering, on the birds or animals he shoots. The aim is always to kill cleanly and to avoid wounding, and shooters always ensure that they have with them a dog or some other means of quickly recovering any quarry that is not killed outright by their shot. Very often, a shooter will give up the opportunity of taking further shots by spending time searching for a wounded bird or animal that he has lost. Shooting is not 'barbaric'. On the contrary, it and the other hunting sports that preceded it, have long existed as a part of many highly civilised societies, including our own. They have added richness and colour to literature, art and music, they have prompted the development of skills in science, technology and engineering, and they continue to do so today. Indeed, the field sports of hunting, shooting and fishing are the core around which complex cultures are based.

There remains, however, the question as to whether it is right for the shooter to kill another creature in the course of what is essentially a recreational activity, and it is a question that everyone who shoots will at some time ask themselves. Before doing so, they should ponder on the fact that life only exists by taking or exploiting other life. Those of us who rely upon other people, such as farmers, to produce the food we eat, the milk we drink or the wool and leather for our clothing and shoes, merely delegate the act of exploiting or killing other animals to somebody else. There is nothing inherently wrong in that, of course. Farmers, on the whole, carry out their task with care and compassion, and to them the cycle of birth and death is part of everyday experience. That natural cycle of birth and death that is so much part of the countryside is fundamental to life itself, and yet modern society has tended to divorce people from it. Not many of us can hope to become farmers. By taking part in field sports such as shooting, however, hundreds of thousands of people are able at least to start to get back in touch with the natural world. Traditionally, most shooters have found their way into the sport because they have followed in the footsteps of their father, uncle or some other family member or friend who has been a keen shooter. If you have no family involvement in shooting or do not live in the countryside, it can often be very difficult to know how to take up the sport, however keen you are to do so.

Shooting successfully at artificial targets is an enormous confidence booster and a challenging and enjoyable form of shooting in its own right, as thousands of competitive clay pigeon shooters will testify.

In fact, there are several common routes into shooting for the enthusiastic newcomer. One of the first ports of call for many people is a local shooting school, the details of which can usually be found on the internet or obtained from one of the shooting associations. Here, you can learn under the guidance of a qualified instructor the art of handling a gun safely and competently. But when you have honed your skills at clay pigeons, then the time may come when you want to move on to sporting shooting in the field, and there are a number of ways in which this can be done. If you are confident in your shooting skills, and absolutely sure of your ability to handle a gun safely, then there are plenty of shooting opportunities available via the internet or advertised in the weekly and monthly shooting magazines. Shooting, whether for game, wildfowl or even woodpigeons, can be bought by the day, or perhaps as part of a package provided by a hotel or guest house. Before booking, check to see that beginners are accepted, that a 'loader' will be available to join you out game shooting or a guide will accompany you on your wildfowling or pigeon shooting trip. In due course, and once you have made friends in the shooting field, you may wish to join a local game shooting syndicate and thereby gain the opportunity to participate in a set number of shooting days each season, and perhaps also to invite one or more of your new-found shooting friends to join you.

There are several routes into shooting for the newcomer.

Make quite clear the fact that you are a novice: nobody will think you the worse for it and, indeed, the overwhelming majority of shooters will be keen and eager to help you.

Another route into shooting is to join a club. Pigeon shooting and rough shooting clubs exist all round the country, and wildfowling clubs control much of the finest wildfowl shooting around our coasts. They organise enjoyable social functions as well as renting or owning land for shooting. Most clubs run clay shoots during the summer, and very often as a member you will be expected to do your bit to assist with countryside management tasks, from building release pens to constructing bridges across the salt marsh. Shooting clubs offer a supportive environment for the novice shooter, and there will generally be members who will be prepared to offer advice and assistance, and to let you accompany them on their shooting trips. Most shooting clubs are affiliated to the BASC, from whom the name of the club secretary or chairman can be obtained. There are also an increasing number of opportunities open to young shooters. All of the national shooting associations, plus many local shooting clubs, hold special training and tuition days for young shots, normally at recognised clay pigeon shooting grounds. Generally, guns and ammunition are provided, and expert tuition and guidance is always on hand. Young shooters' days do not merely provide instruction on shotgun handling. They combine practical shooting tuition with guidance on gun safety and other activities such as air rifle shooting. Details of nationally run instruction days for young or new shooters can be obtained from the BASC, the Countryside Alliance (CA) and the Game and Wildlife Conservation Trust (GWCT). In addition, all these organisations hold

Shooting is a social sport which promotes friendship and companionship.

courses for people of all ages on subjects connected with shooting. These range from shoot management and vermin control courses to gundog training days and wildfowling courses, which provide the opportunity for participants to go shooting under the supervision of experienced wildfowlers. Even if you do not shoot, there are plenty of opportunities to get involved in the shooting scene by offering your services to a local gamekeeper who is looking for beaters or who needs assistance with game rearing during the summer months. Gundog clubs are also ready to welcome new members who are interested in training their dogs for work in the shooting field. There are few better ways of understanding and learning to appreciate the sport of shooting than by getting involved in beating, shoot management and gundog work. There are a number of membership bodies associated with live quarry shooting, but the three principal associations are the BASC, the CA and the GWCT. With 150,000 members, BASC is the largest shooting organisation in Britain. It represents shooting interests at local, national and international levels, and provides a wealth of advice and support to members through its technical departments and regional centres. The CA maintains a wider brief, working on behalf of all field sports and to maintain the social and economic wellbeing of the countryside. The GWCT is a charitable organisation that uses science to promote game and wildlife management as an essential part of nature conservation. Details of these and other organisations can be found in the appendix.

> Everyone who takes part in shooting or its associated activities should be a member of at least one of the national organisations that work on behalf of the sport.

Whether you are just starting on your shooting career or whether you are looking to develop and widen an established interest in shooting, remember that you do not need to look far before finding an experienced shooter prepared to help and guide you in a sport that can provide lifelong interest and enjoyment.

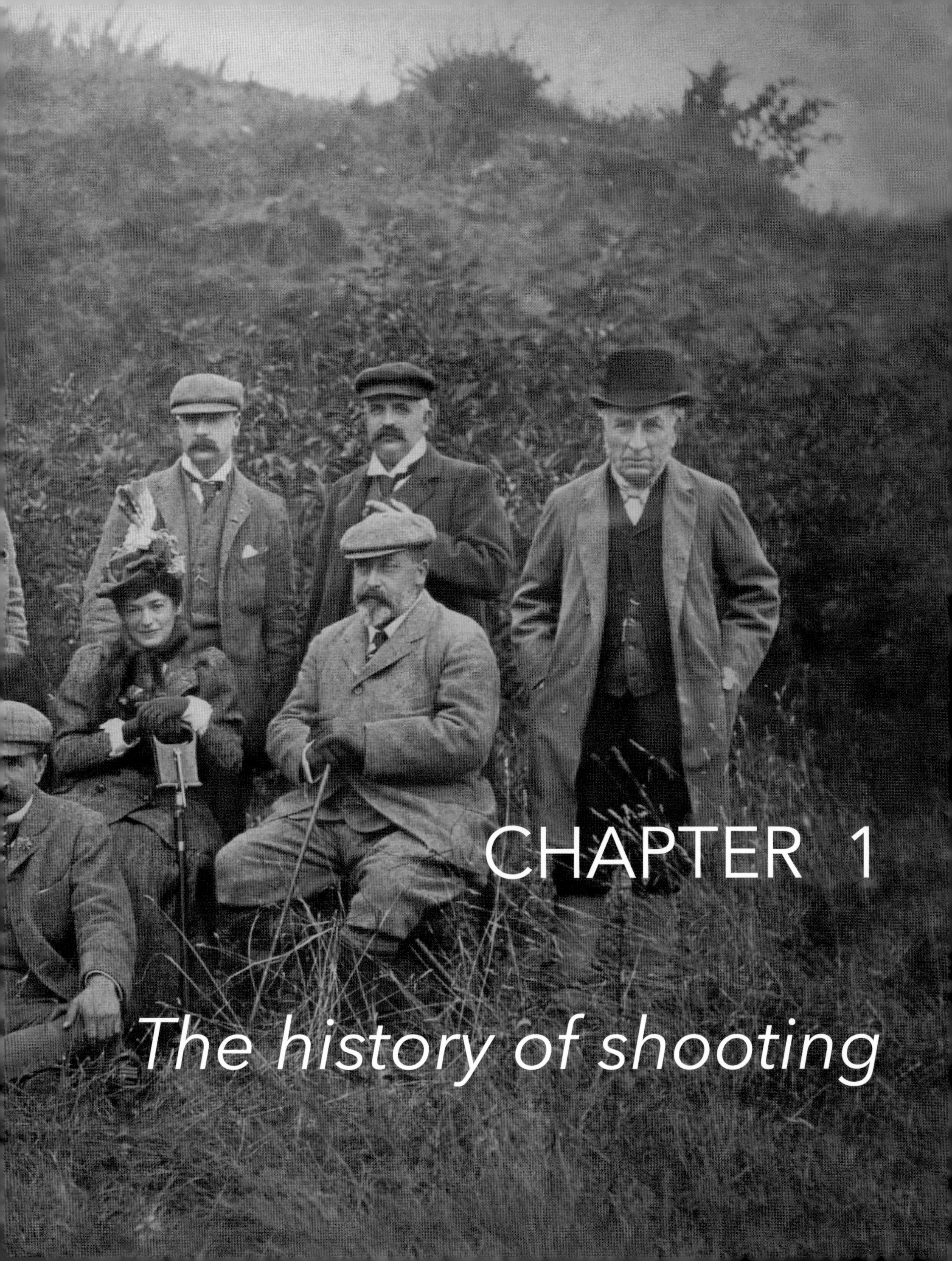

CHAPTER 1

The history of shooting

THE HISTORY OF SHOOTING

SINCE the time that man first walked the Earth, he has been a hunter. Long before human beings ever learned to grow crops and feed themselves and their families by farming the land, they obtained their food by gathering edible plants from the wild, by catching fish and by hunting birds and animals. Although today those of us who live in developed countries no longer need to hunt in order to survive, the hunting instinct remains deep within everyone. Pastimes like shooting, in which modern man can practise traditional hunting skills such as marksmanship, the use of working dogs and the pitting of human wits against those of his quarry, therefore satisfy a universal need.

An eighteenth-century shooter with his pointers. Hunting has been a sport in the developed world for hundreds of years.

Wild food is still a valuable by-product of hunting, and one which is of growing interest both to hunters and non-hunters alike. However, for many hundreds of years, hunting in the developed world has been undertaken mainly because it is enjoyed as a sport or recreation, so just like every other sport, it has developed a complicated code of rules and conventions. In many cases these rules serve to emphasise the importance of hunting skills and the hunter's respect for his quarry. They tip the balance in favour of the hunted bird or animal and render the taking or killing of it more difficult, making the successful hunt more rewarding and satisfying in consequence. For example you will never see a pheasant shooter take a shot at a pheasant that is sitting on the ground. In fact the faster it is flying and the further away it is from the shooter – provided that it is still within range of the gun – the better the shooter likes it. If the objective was simply to kill pheasants the shooter would be far better off shooting them on the ground with a rifle; but it is not. Instead, the modern shooter's main objective is to achieve the satisfaction that comes when a sporting shot has been well executed. For ancient hunters, the main priority must have been to kill sufficient game to guarantee the survival of themselves and their families, but it would be surprising if they too did not also appreciate the excitement of the hunt and the satisfaction which it must have given them.

Hunting in ancient times

Early man soon developed highly complex hunting cultures. Indeed, it is widely accepted that hunting contributed greatly to the development of co-operation between different groups of ancient people, and so became one of the cornerstones of emerging civilisation. To hunt large and dangerous animals like the cave bear, which was extensively pursued in the Old Stone Age or Palaeolithic era, needed teamwork and co-operation between individual hunters. This requirement almost certainly helped to develop the power of language and communication. Hunting also led to the establishment of ritual. Neanderthal hunters living 170,000 years ago in what is now Austria developed a cult in which their quarry, the bear, became an object of religious significance, and late Palaeolithic hunters living between 12,000 and 20,000 years ago decorated the walls and roofs of their caves with magnificent pictures of the animals they hunted. The most famous paintings at the Altamira caves in Spain and the French Lascaux and more recently discovered Chauvet caves near Avignon were probably connected with rituals aimed at ensuring the success of future hunting expeditions, and must certainly have been central to the developing cultures of the communities of people who created them.

Ancient man used several methods to kill his quarry. Spears, traps of all sorts and trained hunting dogs were among the first to appear, and then in the Neolithic period came the bow and arrow. For the first time, hunters had the means to shoot at and kill distant and even fast-moving birds and animals.

These basic tools – the spear, the trap, the hound and the bow and arrow – remained central to hunting for thousands of years, to be joined in due course by trained birds of prey.

The birth of firearms

The invention of gunpowder some time before 1200 was one of the most momentous events in the history of man. Nobody knows exactly who discovered that the mixing of charcoal, saltpetre and sulphur created a powerful explosive, or where the mixture was first made. However, it seems that gunpowder was being used in China for making fireworks long before it was known in the West. The first European to be credited with the manufacture of gunpowder was the Franciscan friar, Roger Bacon, who wrote down the precious formula in about 1250. Before very long, the possibilities of using gunpowder as a propellant had become apparent, and primitive mortars shaped like flower vases were used by the armies of the day to launch rocks and other projectiles at enemy positions.

The earliest handgun, a simple tube closed at one end and mounted on a stick or haft, appeared in the fourteenth century. Though useful as a weapon of war, it was not much good for hunting. It was clumsy and could not be aimed with any accuracy, and, in any case, firing it by means of a smouldering 'match' – a long piece of glowing cord – was such a complex and uncertain process that most birds or animals would have been able to make good their escape long before the shooter could have got anywhere near them to discharge his piece. The bow, the hound and the hawk held sway for another two hundred years before a crucial modification to the basic design of the gun finally enabled aimed shots to be taken with accuracy and some degree of consistency. This development was the creation of the matchlock gun.

WHAT IS GUNPOWDER?

An explosive is a mixture or compound that burns very rapidly and produces a very large volume of gas. All explosives must therefore combine a highly combustible substance with a chemical that produces the necessary oxygen to allow combustion to take place. Gunpowder, which was probably developed in China and the Islamic world long before it became known in Europe, is one of the simplest explosives and consists of saltpetre (potassium nitrate), charcoal and sulphur. When the mixture is ignited, the charcoal and sulphur burn in the oxygen given off by the saltpetre, and the gunpowder produces about 4,000 times its own volume of gas, and a great deal of choking grey smoke.

Gunpowder was originally made in private homes, but the dangers involved in this practice were soon recognised, and in 1461 its manufacture was limited to special places such as the Tower of London. Eventually, gunpowder factories were developed. Because of the ever-present risk of explosion these were built far away from human habitation. Powered by water, they utilised wooden machinery to reduce the risk of accidental ignition.

'Black powder', as gunpowder is now called in order to distinguish it from modern propellants, is a black granular substance, which is supplied in varying degrees of coarseness to users of antique or reproduction muzzle-loading guns. The finer grades burn more quickly and are used in pistols and for priming large guns. Sporting guns require a medium grade, of the consistency of coarse sand. Large guns and cannons use a slower burning coarse grain powder, in which the grains measure 2–3mm across.

Whatever the grain size, black powder burns relatively slowly and progressively, giving a 'gentle shove' up the barrel rather than a 'big kick'. It therefore develops much lower pressures in the chamber than the nitro powders that were developed in the late nineteenth century. Old guns that have been proved only for black powder must never be used with modern cartridges.

The matchlock

The matchlock had two important features. One was the fact that the firing tube – the barrel – was mounted on a shoulder stock, thus enabling the shooter to sight along the top of it. The other was that the

A wildfowler with a matchlock in around 1570. Matchlocks were the first effective hunting weapons.

means of ignition, the slow burning match, was clamped in a curved metal arm called a 'serpentine', which in turn was operated by a lever or trigger. This enabled the match to be applied in a controlled way by the fingers of one hand, to a priming pan containing a small quantity of gunpowder. When the powder in the priming pan ignited, it sent a hot spurt of flame through a touch-hole directly into the main powder charge, thus firing the gun.

For the first time, deliberate shots could be taken at game birds or animals, provided that the shooter was able to stalk within range, and it was not long before the matchlock gun developed to a high degree of sophistication. These guns were elaborate and costly, so were available only to the wealthier classes of society. But it was clear that the idea of stalking game, and more particularly wildfowl, had taken hold amongst the common people, for in 1533 Henry VIII passed an act that forbade anyone to shoot with any handgun unless they had land worth £100 a year, a great deal of money in those days. Henry, himself a shooting enthusiast, was obviously concerned to restrict the new sport to the better off, and to ensure that the menfolk of England did not neglect the practice of archery with their longbows, a skill that in the period was of vital importance to the nation in time of war.

Firearms were not so easily put down, however, and early gunmakers eagerly sought to improve their products. Particular attention was paid to the method of ignition, for the slow-burning match was by no means ideal. In wet or windy weather the glowing cord would all too easily be extinguished, while if a matchlock was used for hunting game, the burning match would frequently alert the quarry to the shooter's presence.

The wheel-lock

The first mechanical means of igniting a firearm came with the invention of the wheel-lock. This employed a clockwork system that was used to drive a mechanism rather like the one that could be found in a cigarette lighter. At the centre of the wheel-lock was a serrated steel wheel, which could be made to spin round when the trigger was pressed. A piece of iron pyrites, held in the jaws of a 'cock', was forced against the fast-revolving wheel, sending a shower of sparks into the priming pan and so firing the gun. Although wheel-locks became popular in Germany and Eastern Europe where a robust version known as the *Tschinke* was developed to withstand rough handling in the field, they never achieved wide acceptance in England.

Hunters with wheel-lock guns in 1582.

The main reason for this was that the wheel-lock was a very complex, delicate and thus expensive piece of engineering. It was also one that was largely unsuited to the demands of the hunter. So the wheel-lock remained principally a weapon of war and more particularly a tool of the mounted soldier. Most everyday people stuck with their old-fashioned matchlocks, and after the English Civil War of the 1640s large numbers of matchlocks came into circulation and were widely used by hunters to shoot game and wildfowl.

Flint and steel

Meanwhile, gunmakers were constantly on the lookout for new methods of ignition, and eventually they turned to flint and steel in order to fire their weapons. The earliest form of flintlock, known as the 'snaphance' after the Dutch word *snaphaan* or snapping cockerel, appeared in the middle of the sixteenth century. It had a cock containing a flint, which struck a moving steel or 'frizzen'. To operate the snaphance, the shooter first had to slide the cover off the priming pan and ensure that the frizzen was set and the cock drawn fully back. When the shooter pulled the trigger, the flint struck the frizzen, which moved smartly backwards allowing the sparks to fall into the open pan.

It was certainly an advance on the old wheel-lock, but it still required the shooter to open the priming pan manually before he fired, so exposing the priming powder to wind and weather and preventing the taking of anything but slow, deliberate shots. That all changed with the invention of the true flintlock in the first quarter of the seventeenth century. In the flintlock, the frizzen and pan cover were joined together into an L-shaped component that flipped back when it was struck a glancing blow by the flint, opening the pan to receive its shower of hot sparks, and so allowing the gun to be fired.

For two hundred years the flintlock reigned supreme. Gunmakers across Europe developed and perfected it into a weapon that was both elegantly engineered and beautiful to look at. In fact, the lines of the later flintlock are broadly similar to those of the modern sporting gun, and the age of the flintlock saw the birth of famous gunmaking firms such as James Purdey & Sons, who are still in business today.

Left: When the flint of a flintlock strikes the frizzen, a shower of hot sparks is thrown into the priming pan, causing the priming powder to ignite. This, in turn, sets off the main powder charge and fires the gun.

Below: A flintlock shotgun from around 1800, by Fowler of Dublin. The familiar appearance of the sporting shotgun was established by this time and many of its characteristics are still with us today.

The advent of the flintlock enabled sportsmen to shoot flying quarry.

The flintlock was reasonably weatherproof, easy to load and fire, pretty reliable provided that it was kept clean and the flint regularly replaced, and most importantly, it offered much faster ignition than any system that preceded it.

This meant that for the first time shooters had the real chance of being able to shoot birds in flight. Until this time shooting had been an activity undertaken largely by ordinary people who stalked and killed birds for food, while the upper classes stuck mostly to their hounds and hawks. With the arrival of *pteryplegia* or wing-shooting, there was renewed interest in shooting amongst all classes of society and suddenly it became an accepted and fashionable sport in its own right.

The percussion system

The next great revolution in gunmaking occurred in 1807, when a Scottish clergyman called Alexander Forsyth patented a means of firing a gun by using a detonating powder. This was a chemical compound that exploded when a small quantity of it was struck a direct blow. Although it caused too violent an explosion for it to be suitable for use as a propellant, it was found to be a perfect alternative to flint and steel in igniting a conventional charge of gunpowder.

At first, Forsyth's invention was dismissed by conservative shooters, who preferred to stick to their trusty flintlocks. But before long, the benefits of the detonating system became obvious. In particular, it was much more reliable than the flintlock in wet weather, when the old fashioned flint and steel was particularly prone to misfiring. So before long, gunmakers rushed to develop the best way of applying the detonating principle to the sporting gun. By the time that Forsyth's patent expired in 1821, the true percussion shotgun was born.

Instead of the side-mounted priming pan of the flintlock, the standard percussion shotgun has a small tube or 'nipple' that leads directly down into the chamber where the powder charge is located. A small copper cap, containing a tiny quantity of detonating material, is placed over the top of the nipple. When struck by the hammer of the gun a jet of very hot flame is sent straight into the centre of the powder, thereby igniting it evenly and quickly. Vast numbers of these guns were made, while equal numbers of flintlocks were converted to

The percussion shotgun was loaded from the muzzle but ignited by a copper cap placed over a hollow tubular nipple. The cap detonated when struck by the hammer, sending a jet of flame into the charge, thus firing the gun.

For a while, sporting shotguns continued to use external hammers, and indeed, the 'hammer gun' can still be seen in use today. One of its benefits is that because the hammers have to be drawn back or 'cocked' before the gun is fired, it is plain to see when the gun is in the ready-to-fire condition. Likewise, when the hammers are at rest, the gun is seen to be relatively safe. But using a hammer gun also has disadvantages. It is necessary to cock both hammers before you can shoot, and this takes time, even for the most practised shooter. Hammers can also get caught in twigs or barbed wire, maybe leading to the gun discharging accidentally. In the 1870s, gunmakers developed the 'hammerless' gun in which the firing mechanism was contained within the body of the action and the external hammers were discarded. No longer was there any need to draw the hammers back by hand, and in most hammerless guns, the action is cocked automatically when the barrels are opened for reloading. By the mid-1880s the hammerless gun had achieved a measure of dominance, although hammer guns continued to be manufactured for many more years to come.

A double-barrelled 12-bore hammer gun. Guns of this type achieved universal popularity and some are still in use today.

The nineteenth century was a period that saw more changes and developments in firearms technology than any other, most of them driven by the constant need for improved military smallarms. One of the most important of these was the introduction of mass production. For the first time, it became possible to replace expensive and time-consuming hand labour with machine manufacture, thus opening up the way to the production of cheaper guns. Spurred on by the rapidly developing market for sporting firearms both at home and in the colonies, gunmakers worked feverishly on every conceivable idea in order to perfect the shotgun. Further refinements swiftly followed, such as the introduction of an ejector mechanism to expel the spent cartridge cases from the breech, and the development of the single trigger, which could, if required, be used to replace the conventional double triggers on a double-barrelled gun. By the dawn of the twentieth century, the evolution of the classic sporting shotgun was virtually complete.

New propellants

Alongside the development of the shotgun ran that of the explosive propellant that was used in it. We have seen how the recipe for gunpowder, or 'black powder', as it is known, was written down in the middle of the thirteenth century. Early powder was crude and unreliable. It burned slowly, and so a significant amount of time was needed from the moment of ignition to the point at which the powder charge developed its full pressure. Because of this, early guns had very long barrels to accommodate the progressive combustion of the propellant. By the end of the eighteenth century, military necessity had brought the manufacture of black powder to a fine art. It was made commercially in special water-powered powder mills where the risk of explosion could be kept to an absolute minimum. But black powder still remained a messy explosive to use. In particular, it left large quantities of sulphurous black fouling behind after it was fired and it produced great clouds of grey smoke. Soon, industrial chemists were busy at work finding alternatives.

Their searches centred on the new 'nitro' compounds that are formed when cellulose material such as cotton is treated with nitric acid. Pioneers like Alfred Nobel eventually formulated explosive materials that were stable and safe enough for use in firearms, and before long the dirty, smoky, black powder gave way to the smokeless, fast-burning nitro powders we use today.

In seven hundred years, thanks to the ingenuity of countless gunmakers, the primitive 'hand-gonne', which was probably just as dangerous to its user as it was to its intended target, has been transformed into the sleek, elegant sporting shotgun we know today. Shooting has been made safe and efficient, while the mass manufacture of shotguns has brought the sport within reach of millions of people.

SUPER STAR
200st/pcs
Lerduvor

CHAPTER 2

Shotguns and cartridges

SHOTGUNS AND CARTRIDGES

WHETHER you wish to shoot game or clay targets, whether you want to pursue wildfowl on the salt marsh, woodpigeons on the fields at harvest time or grouse on the moors, you will require a shotgun.

What is a shotgun? Put quite simply, it is a weapon designed to shoot a charge of small pellets, normally at a moving target. Every aspect of its construction is geared towards helping the shooter place an even and consistent pattern of shot on his selected target time and time again. At the heart of the shotgun is a powerful spring that works the lock, and that is compressed when the gun is cocked. This normally happens when the barrels are dropped down for loading. Pulling the trigger releases the spring, which throws forward the striker to make contact with the cartridge. The primer is ignited and in an instant the powder charge contained within the cartridge explodes, shooting the wad and shot up the barrel ahead of a rapidly expanding column of hot gases.

Lock, stock and barrel

A shotgun is described as a smooth-bore weapon. This means that unlike a rifle, which has a series of spiral grooves down its barrel

An over-and-under shotgun open and ready for loading. Note the top lever which has been pushed to the right to open the gun, and the safety catch, which is on 'safe'. Pushing the catch forward, once the gun is loaded and closed, will make it ready for firing.

to impart a steadying spin to the bullet, it has barrel walls that are absolutely smooth. Look through the barrel of an empty shotgun and you will see that the inside of it is highly polished. This ensures that any damage or distortion that may be caused to the shot pellets as they travel up the tube is kept to an absolute minimum. Perfectly spherical pellets fly straight and true through the air; damaged ones do not, and so decrease the shooter's chance of killing his quarry or breaking his clay target.

The 'action' of a shotgun is the section of it that contains most of the working parts that enable the gun to be cocked and fired. Like the barrel, the action is finely and carefully engineered to withstand the enormous pressures that are generated when the gun is fired. Fitted to the action is the stock, traditionally made of walnut but today often moulded from high-density plastic, which enables the shooter to mount the gun snugly to his shoulder.

Apart from 'lock, stock and barrel', there are a number of fundamental parts or working controls that are to be found on the conventional shotgun. Below the barrels is the fore-end, which may contain within it those working parts that operate the ejector mechanism, designed to throw spent cartridges clear of the breech automatically when the gun is opened. When the fore-end is detached, the barrels can be removed easily from the stock and action.

Most guns have an automatic safety catch that engages on 'safe' when the gun is opened for reloading. However, some do not, and special care must be taken with guns that have a manual safety catch. Beneath the action will be found the trigger or triggers. A single-barrelled gun will obviously have only one trigger. Older double-barrelled guns often have two triggers, the front one normally operating the right barrel and the back one the left barrel. However, modern double-barrelled guns are more likely to be fitted with a single trigger, usually with a selector to enable the shooter to choose which barrel he wishes to fire first. Around

Most modern shotguns are opened or 'broken' by means of a top lever, to be found on top of the action. When pushed smartly to the right, the barrels drop down to enable the gun to be loaded. Immediately behind it can usually be found the safety catch. This locks the triggers and prevents the gun from being fired, although the safety catch should never be relied upon, and no gun is ever 'safe' unless it is unloaded.

the triggers is a curved trigger guard to prevent the triggers from being snagged and the gun fired accidentally.

Different types of shotgun

The ingenuity and inventiveness of generations of gunmakers and the demands of sportsmen for ever better weapons has led to the development of an almost bewildering variety of shotguns. To the collector or the firearms enthusiast, the study of shotguns and the appreciation of their engineering and artistry can become a lifelong study. Yet, there are a number of distinct types which every shooter will recognise.

Double-barrelled shotguns

Best known of all shotguns is the double-barrelled shotgun in which the barrels are either superimposed one on top of the other or placed

An over-and-under shotgun by Boxall & Edmiston. Superbly crafted shotguns like this are still made by the English gun trade.

side by side. While the side-by-side shotgun enjoyed over two hundred years of popularity and a close association with the sport of game shooting, it is the over-and-under shotgun that is favoured by today's shooters for its strong action, narrow sighting plane and excellent 'pointability'. Guns with superimposed barrels have been produced in small numbers by Europe's gunmakers for centuries, but it was the adoption of the over-and-under shotgun by the competition shooting world that led to it becoming what it is today, the overwhelming favourite of all shooters worldwide. Nevertheless, you will often still see the more traditional side-by-side shotgun in use, especially on game shoots.

Sometimes, these will be hand-made guns of very high quality, great beauty and perhaps considerable age. The English gun trade has long been associated with such exquisite products, and a small number of firms continue to produce magnificently crafted shotguns, the component parts usually being precision made before the guns are hand assembled and finished. However, the combined output of the UK gun trade is nowadays no more than a few hundred shotguns a year, and the vast majority of guns on sale in dealers' premises are factory made and imported.

The side-by-side shotgun still enjoys great popularity in the game shooting field.

Right and below: Whether for clays or live quarry, the over-and-under shotgun is overwhelmingly favoured by today's shooters.

Above left: Finishing a fine shotgun at the Boxall & Edmiston factory. Hundreds of hours of work go into the manufacture of a fine shotgun.

Above right: The stock of a shotgun may be altered or modified to suit the shooter's physique or shooting style. This gun has a 'cross-over' stock that enables a shooter with limited vision in his right eye to shoot off his right shoulder.

Single-barrelled shotguns

Single-barrelled shotguns are widely used in all forms of sporting shooting and, like their double-barrelled cousins, come in a variety of different forms. Perhaps the simplest is the basic 'break action' shotgun, which has been the workhorse of generations of gamekeepers, rough shooters and young shots. Cheap, rugged and reliable, the single-barrelled gun is often selected as a first shotgun for the novice, and very good it is too, despite its obvious shortcomings.

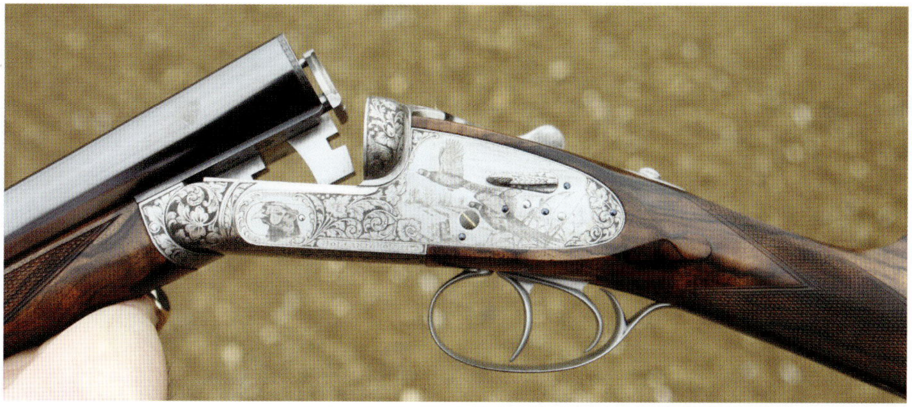

Left: The 'best' sidelock is still regarded as the pinnacle of fine gunmaking and, as with this Holland & Holland shotgun, provides every opportunity for the engraver to express his artistry.

When a shotgun is fired, the rapid expansion of gases produced by the exploding propellant force the wad out of the barrel, driving the shot ahead of it in a tightly packed column. In this picture, the shot can be seen travelling towards a clay target.

Magazine shotguns

Magazine shotguns have the ability to fire multiple shots without further cartridges being manually introduced into the chamber. This category includes both the pump-action and the semi-automatic shotgun.

- Pump-action shotguns have a cylindrical magazine situated below the barrel. After a shot has been taken, a single back and forth 'pumping' motion of the fore-end ejects the spent cartridge case, loads a fresh round into the chamber and cocks the gun at the same time.

- In a semi-automatic, the process of feeding a round from the magazine into the chamber is done automatically, either by utilising the propellant gases or the recoil from the preceding shot. All the shooter has to do is to pull the trigger.

Because they do not have to be broken for reloading, magazine shotguns are particularly popular amongst pigeon shooters, wildfowlers and pest controllers who shoot from confined hides. Furthermore, they are simple in design and manufacture, extremely rugged and

The semi-automatic shotgun is a popular choice amongst wildfowlers and pigeon shooters.

ideal for those shooters who need a cheap, reliable workhorse of a gun. And because part of its recoil energy is used to work the reloading mechanism, the semi-automatic has a particularly low sensible recoil.

However, particular care must be taken with magazine shotguns, because when you are shooting in company you cannot 'break' your gun as you can with a conventional break-action shotgun to demonstrate to those shooting alongside you that the pump-action or semi-automatic is unloaded and thus safe. For this reason, magazine shotguns are not favoured when shooting in the company of other people. In addition, the value of magazine shotguns is restricted by the law, which states that, if they are to be held on a shotgun certificate, they may hold no more than two rounds in the magazine in addition to one in the chamber. This gives the shooter no more than three shots before he has to reload.

Bolt action

The bolt action is more widely associated with rifles than it is with shotguns. Even so, the single-shot bolt-action principle can readily be adapted to shotgun manufacture, and very large numbers of bolt-action shotguns are in use, especially in the smaller calibres such as the .410 or 'four-ten'. To load a bolt-action shotgun, a cartridge is slid into the open breech, after which the bolt is pushed forwards and locked with a downwards rotation of the bolt lever. After firing, the cycle is reversed, the bolt lever being pushed upwards and the bolt drawn back to expel the empty cartridge case. Though it is essentially a simple system, effective operation of the bolt action requires practice, and it is not the ideal gun for the beginner.

Combination guns

Popular in continental Europe are combination guns in which shotgun and rifle barrels are paired together. Such guns are especially suitable where a hunter may encounter both small and large game – such as deer or wild boar – during the course of a day. There is an almost infinite choice of barrel sizes and configurations, with large- and small-calibre rifle barrels being placed under, over or beside one or two shotgun barrels, though among the best known is the 'drilling', which comprises two shotgun barrels with a rifle barrel beneath.

Shotgun calibres

Whereas rifle calibres are normally measured in millimetres or decimals of an inch, shotguns are gauged by bore size. Bore sizes hark back to the days when smooth-bore guns were used to fire single lead musket balls, and the number of the bore size corresponds to the number of balls of pure lead, each exactly fitting the bore of the gun, which together weigh one pound. So a perfectly spherical ball of lead weighing 1oz or 1⁄16lb, will fit exactly into a 16-bore barrel. Likewise, a ball weighing one twelfth of a pound will fit a 12-bore. Thus, the higher the number of the bore size, the smaller its dimension.

By far the most popular bore size worldwide is the 12-bore. However, the smaller gauge shotguns have grown markedly in popularity in recent years amongst game shooters. Young shots and women shooters also often prefer the smaller 20- or 28-bore shotguns, with their light shot loads and consequently lower recoil. The less frequently encountered 16-bore is a halfway house between the 20- and the 12-bore, but, nevertheless, has its small band of strong supporters, especially in continental Europe. At the other end of the scale, the large-bore shotguns comprise the 10-bore, the 8-bore and the massive 4-bore. Such guns are rarely encountered outside the specialised field of wildfowling and in particular goose shooting, where they are used to deliver large charges of heavy shot at extreme range.

Large-bore shotguns such as this mighty 4-bore hammer gun are a rare sight, but are still used by some specialist goose shooters.

Two small and commonly encountered shotgun gauges are measured like rifle calibres in inches or millimetres. The .410 is valuable for vermin control and is a traditional calibre for children learning to shoot. However, the very small charge of shot that it is capable of firing makes the .410 useful only at ranges of up to about 25 metres, and consistent success with a .410 calls for very accurate marksmanship. In truth, the young newcomer to shooting is better off moving directly to one of the larger calibres, such as the 28-bore or, if he or she can manage it, the 20-bore. Smaller even than the .410 is the 9mm or 'Number 3 garden gun'. This is useful for dealing with small vermin such as rats or mice in confined spaces, but it has little value as a sporting weapon.

Shotgun cartridge gauges, from left to right: .410, 28-bore, 20-bore, 16-bore, 12-bore, 10-bore, 8-bore, 4-bore.

Cartridges

Just as there is a very wide range of shotguns available to the sporting shooter, so the variety of cartridges appears almost limitless. However, the basic design of the centre-fire shotgun cartridge is extremely simple. A cartridge, in essence, contains three things:

- explosive powder together with a means of ignition
- a wad column to act as a piston
- a charge of shot.

The expertise of ballisticians and cartridge manufacturers has refined these ingredients to the point at which a huge range of different cartridges are now available for any type of shooting.

The propellant powder – gunpowder has long been replaced by smokeless powders of various sorts – is ignited by the primer, which sits in its own small chamber in the base of the cartridge. When hit by the striker of the shotgun, the primer directs a hot burst of flame into the powder charge, which has to burn cleanly and uniformly to accelerate the shot out of the barrel. A variety of powders exist, enabling the cartridge manufacturer to design loads that give the shot everything from a short, hard kick to a relatively long, slow push up the barrel. Seated on top of the powder, the wad has a vital role to perform in transferring the energy of the propellant to the shot charge. Traditionally, wads were cut from thick organic felt or fibrous material, but in recent years the plastic wad has been widely adopted. This may have a shot cup to protect the shot from abrasion against the barrel wall, thus helping to ensure that a better, more even pattern of shot strikes the target. However, plastic wads have one major disadvantage in that they do not easily biodegrade. Neither can they easily be picked up by hand like spent cartridge cases. Where a great deal of shooting takes place, a build up of spent plastic wads can occur, which both looks unsightly and can prove dangerous to grazing farm animals.

For this reason, many clay pigeon grounds and game shoots require the use of the traditional fibre wad.

Shot size

Shot comes in a variety of different sizes, from the smallest conventional size 9 (2mm) to LG (9.1mm) shot, which is used against heavy game such as wild boar. The lower the number, the larger the shot size, and the most commonly used sizes for live quarry shooting are 4, 5, 6 and 7. For pheasants, partridges and other game birds, most shooters will prefer sizes 6 or 7. The slightly larger size 5 is often preferred for use against rabbits, and for shooting hares, size 4 can be very effective. Goose shooters use even larger shot sizes, such as 3, 1 or BB, while at the other end of the scale, specialist snipe shooters opt for size 8. The standard game load for a 12-bore shotgun is 30g ($1^{1}/_{16}$ oz) of size 6 shot, containing 287 pellets.

Most shot used for shooting upland game is made from lead. However, some birds, especially waterfowl, can be at risk from lead poisoning if they eat spent lead pellets from areas that are regularly shot over and in many countries, including the UK, legislation is in place that requires shooters to use non-lead shot when shooting in wetland areas or when shooting wildfowl. When using non-lead shot, and especially steel shot, it is very important to ensure that the type of cartridge you choose is suitable for your gun.

SHOT SIZES

		Diameter	
		mm	in
	LG	9.1	.36
	SG	8.4	.33
	Spec SG	7.6	.30
	SSG	6.8	.27
	AAA	5.2	.20
	BB	4.1	.16
	1	3.6	.14
	3	3.3	.13
	4	3.1	.12
	5	2.8	.11
	6	2.6	.10
	7	2.4	.095
	7½	2.3	.09
	8	2.2	.085
	9	2.0	.08

such as the heart or lungs, with the shock of a multiple strike of pellets. To kill a particular quarry consistently, the shooter therefore has to ensure that sufficient pellets hit the target on every occasion, and that the pellets have enough energy to cause that shock and vital damage. This in itself dictates the effective range of a shotgun and cartridge.

Because pellets spread more widely the further they get from the muzzle of the gun, and because larger pellets retain their energy further downrange than small ones, the shooter who chooses a cartridge containing a small number of large pellets will find that there is a point at which his pattern becomes too thin to ensure that the target is struck by sufficient pellets to kill it. Although each pellet still retains sufficient energy to inflict vital damage, the chance of a pellet actually striking a vital spot is remote. Sometimes, you may hear a shooter boast about a bird that was killed with a single pellet at very great range. In fact, the success of such shots is down to nothing more than luck.

Likewise, the shooter who uses a cartridge containing a large number of small pellets will find a point at which, even if the shot is centred upon the target, the pellets have insufficient energy to cause enough shock to kill the quarry. Although the bird or animal may be struck by several pellets, even the combination of all of them will still not be lethal. Individual pellets may, however, cause wounding, and the quarry may fly or run on to die later from its injuries. No good sporting shooter will shoot at a quarry that he knows to be out of range for the gun and cartridge that he is using.

The ability to judge range instinctively and a sure knowledge of the capabilities of your gun and cartridge are fundamental to good shooting.

Choke

There is, however, a modification that is fitted to or incorporated within most shotgun barrels that regulates the density of the shot pattern independently of range. This is known as 'choke'. A choked barrel is slightly constricted in the last few centimetres before the muzzle. This constriction concentrates or squeezes the shot as it emerges from the barrel and so produces a tighter pattern. This ensures that there is more chance of several pellets striking the target when a shot is taken at longer range.

VARIABLE CHOKE

When a conventional shotgun barrel is manufactured, the internal diameter of the bore is usually very slightly reduced in the last few centimetres nearest the muzzle in order to provide the 'choke' or constriction that helps to hold the shot pellets closer together in flight, so producing a tighter pattern. Once the gun has been completed, it is possible – though expensive – for a gunsmith to alter the choke. However, because such alteration involves taking away metal from the inside of the bore, choke can only be removed from a gun; never added to it.

Many shooters find that they prefer different degrees of choke for different types of shooting. They may, for example want a tight choke when the targets that they are intending to shoot are likely to be at longer range, and then to switch to a more open choke to shoot at closer range targets without necessarily changing to a different gun. Gunmakers have therefore developed the variable choke system.

There are a number of variants of this system on the market, but all involve the use of carefully engineered choke tubes, which may be screwed into the muzzle of the gun. To accommodate these tubes, the inside of the muzzle must be cut with a screw thread. The shooter will normally have a set of tubes, ranging from open chokes delivering even patterns at short ranges to full or extra-full chokes producing tight patterns for long range shooting. Choke tubes are fitted to the gun with a special wrench. They may be marked with a pattern of notches in the end, so that the shooter can easily tell which choke he has fitted.

Variable choke thus offers added flexibility to the shooter who only has one gun but wishes to enjoy a wide range of different types of shooting with it.

Choke tubes.

There are five recognised degrees of choke: full choke, half-choke, three-quarter choke, quarter-choke and improved cylinder.

A barrel without any choke at all is said to be true cylinder. A more tightly choked barrel may have slightly greater effective range than a cylinder barrel, but the shooter, accordingly, must be more accurate in placing the smaller shot pattern squarely on target. Most double-barrelled shotguns with fixed chokes have one barrel more tightly choked than the other. In a side-by-side shotgun the left barrel is normally choked more tightly than the right, while in an over and under shotgun, the top barrel usually has more choke than the bottom one. Many modern guns are fitted with a variable choke system, by which a choke cone with the required degree of constriction may be selected and then screwed into the muzzle of the gun with a special key. If you are at all unsure about which choke to use and which shot size to select, always opt for the more open choke and the smaller shot size, and take only the targets that are well within range. There is no dishonour in not shooting at a bird because you think it may be out of range, and in time you will learn to appreciate and understand the capabilities of your gun.

Cleaning and maintenance

Your gun should be properly looked after. If it is well cared for, regularly maintained and cleaned after use, then a well built gun may last a lifetime or more. If neglected it will soon deteriorate, lose its value and even become dangerous both to its user and to other people. Cleaning a gun is a very simple process, which anybody can do immediately after returning from shooting.

When shooting in wet weather, it is a good idea to take an absorbent cloth with you to wipe your gun down after shooting. A quick spray over the metalwork with an aerosol gun oil before putting it in its slip will ensure that it has not started to develop rust spots by the time you arrive home. Then, before you start to clean the gun, warm it through by placing it near a gentle heat source such as a radiator. Alternatively, you may use a hair dryer over it. This will drive off any remaining moisture from the gun before you start to clean it. Although you may in time learn how to carry out simple repairs to your gun, it is far better at first to leave even basic maintenance to the experts. Always remember to take your gun to an experienced gunsmith for an annual overhaul, preferably soon after the close of the shooting season. He will strip the gun down, correct any minor faults and tell you if he thinks that there is anything that requires more serious work. It is far better to get any potential problems put right at this stage than to have a fault develop while you are out shooting, perhaps with disastrous consequences.

A typical shotgun cleaning kit consisting of a sectioned cleaning rod, a jag, a phosphor bronze brush and an absorbent mop, gun oil in both liquid and aerosol forms, cleaning patches and a pair of gunsmith's turnscrews.

CLEANING THE GUN

1. First, the gun should be dismantled by removing the fore-end and detaching the barrels from the action.
2. Immediately wipe off any moisture with an absorbent cloth or a piece of kitchen roll, before getting to work on the barrels.
3. With a mop fitted to the end of your cleaning rod, briskly brush any burnt powder deposit out of the bore.
4. Then remove the mop and brush the bore with a phosphor bronze brush to remove any traces of lead.
5. Finally, using a jag and a cleaning patch with a little gun oil on it, smear the inside of the bore with a thin film of oil.
6. When the barrels are clean inside, wipe the outsides with an oil-soaked patch, being careful to remove any debris from under the ejectors. Hold the barrels carefully. Sticky fingermarks will leave traces of salt on the metal, and this can in time cause rusting to occur.
7. Turning next to the action, wipe the metalwork down carefully with an oily patch, taking care to oil beneath the top lever. Do not squirt oil into every hole or aperture, as this will in time gum up the works when the oil dries and hardens. Neither should you put excessive amounts of gun oil onto the stock, as this will cause the wood to go soft at the point where it is fitted to the body of the action.
8. However, a small amount of linseed or walnut oil is good for the stock and fore-end, especially after they have become soaked on a wet day.

CHAPTER 3

Gun safety

GUN SAFETY

THERE is only one rule that every shooter must unfailingly obey at all times. No matter whether it be in the field, in the home or while travelling, the fundamental rule of shooting is gun safety.

Although they may be designed to kill, guns are nothing more than complicated pieces of metal and wood or plastic, fixed together in a certain way. They are not by themselves dangerous, for no gun ever shot anyone or anything without outside assistance. There is, therefore, no reason for guns to be feared, but they must always be respected. This respect is the guiding principle behind gun safety. It involves knowing and understanding exactly what a gun is capable of doing, and ensuring that it is only permitted to do it when you, the shooter, want it to.

Always be aware of where the muzzles of your gun are pointing in relation to your surroundings.

Handling a shotgun

The shotgun's task is to fire a lethal charge of shot. However, it is not able to do this if it is not loaded, and so the first rule when handling a gun is to check it to see whether or not it contains a cartridge. Whenever you pick up a gun or are passed one by somebody else, the first thing that you must do, always and without fail, even if you believe the gun to be empty, is to open and check it. This reaction to open and check your gun must become instinctive and automatic. It takes only a moment to drop down the barrels on a conventional shotgun, or to check the breech and chamber if it is a semi-automatic, and the couple of seconds taken to do so is time well spent. Apart from providing you with the vital information you need as to whether or not the gun is loaded, it will mark you out, when shooting in company, as someone who understands how to handle a gun safely.

When passing a gun to someone else, it must always be unloaded, and it is up to you to demonstrate that this is so by opening it and passing it, stock first, so that the recipient can see the empty breech. If, for whatever reason, you are passed an unopened gun, then you must immediately open and check it. It does not matter if the person who has passed it to you tells you that it is unloaded; check it anyway.

Unless your gun is open, there is no way in which anyone else will be able to determine whether or not it is unloaded. It is therefore up to you to ensure that, when closed, it is never pointed at anyone or

GUN HANDLING CHECKLIST

1. Check your gun when you pick it up.
2. Check it before you put it down.
3. Check it when passing it to someone and when receiving it.
4. Check it before putting it in its slip and when you get it out again.
5. Check it before putting it into a vehicle or bringing it into a house, and when you take it out again.
6. Check it before starting to clean it, and before putting it away in its security cabinet.
7. Whenever you are in doubt as to whether or not your gun is loaded, check it. Even if you are not in doubt, check it. If you do this, at all times and under all circumstances, then you are well on the way to become a safe gun handler.

anything that you do not intend to shoot. You must develop what is called 'muzzle awareness'. Always be conscious of where those muzzles are pointing in relation to the people, animals and objects round about you. Ensure that under no circumstances, however fleeting, do they pass across another person.

Even though you know it to be empty, because of course you have just checked it, always handle your gun as though it is loaded. Having a gun pointed at you, however accidentally, is a peculiarly unnerving experience, and the shooter who consistently allows his muzzles to wander where they should not will soon be marked out as someone who is unsafe. He or she will soon find that they are not welcome to shoot in the company of other people.

Carrying a gun

There has been much debate over the years as to whether a shotgun should, in company, be carried open or closed. Many older shooters were brought up to carry their guns closed, and maintain that to do so places less strain on the action. Even today, you will see some shooters walking or standing around in company with closed guns. Do not copy them. The only way to carry a shotgun when you are with other people is open, unloaded, and held over the crook of the forearm. If you do this, then those standing next to you will be instantly aware that your gun is safe, and they will be put at their ease.

On a clay shooting ground, if a person walks around with a closed shotgun which is not securely fastened in a gun slip, then they will be very quickly told to open it, and if they do not do so, then they will not find themselves shooting on that ground again.

There is a clear difficulty here with self-loading and pump-action shotguns, for however safe the handler may be, it will not always be immediately obvious to a bystander that the gun itself is empty. Some users of self-loading guns carry with them a cartridge-shaped plug, which has attached to it a coloured ribbon. When this is placed in the chamber, with the ribbon hanging out of the loading port, the gun is demonstrated to be empty. Such a device is useful, but even so, the only infallible rule is to ensure that, when carrying a self-loading shotgun

Carrying a shotgun over the forearm, broken and unloaded.

in company, the receiver is always kept open and the barrel pointed in a safe direction.

Safety in the shooting field

With the principles of gun safety established, let us now look at how a shotgun should be handled in the field. To start with, when you arrive at the place where you will be shooting, be it a farmyard from where you will be departing for a walk along the hedgerows in search of rabbits and pigeons, or your numbered 'peg' on a formal driven shoot, you will remove your gun from its slip.

Break your gun when putting it into its slip, or when removing it.

Removing the gun from its slip

1. To do so, unfasten the slip and withdraw the stock of the gun until you reach the top lever.
2. Then, with the barrels still in the slip, open the gun and withdraw it completely with the barrels in the broken position.
3. Likewise, when you are returning your gun to its slip at the end of the drive or after shooting has been completed, do so with the gun broken, closing the gun only when the barrels are safely within the slip.

Loading the gun

1. Before loading your gun at the start of a drive or a day's shooting, look down the barrels to make sure that there is no obstruction in them.
2. Load a shotgun with the barrels pointing at the ground in front of you with your finger well away from the trigger.
3. If your gun has a manual (non-automatic) safety, then make sure the safety catch is engaged in the 'safe' position.
4. Having placed the cartridge or cartridges in the breech, close the gun by bringing the stock up to meet the barrels. This ensures that as the breech snaps shut, the muzzles are still directed at the ground.

Once you have started walking in search of a shot, or when you have reached your appointed position and are waiting for your quarry to come past you, you will be doing so with a gun that is both loaded and closed, ready to fire. Therefore the barrels will have to be pointed in a safe direction, and this will be done if you either hold the gun over the crook of the forearm, with the muzzles pointing at the ground, or alternatively if you hold it 'at the ready', with the muzzles pointing up into the air.

These positions are acceptable when the shooter is either standing or walking. In addition, some shooters find it comfortable when walking-up game, especially over rough ground, to carry the gun over their shoulder, trigger guard upwards, with the barrels pointing safely into the air above them.

At all times you should ensure that the safety catch is engaged until the moment you raise the gun to your shoulder in order to take a shot. A conventional safety catch, mounted on the top strap of the gun, will be 'safe' when it is in the rearwards position. Normally this will expose an engraved or inlaid 'safe' or 'S'. Try to get into the habit of sliding the safety catch forward as part of the act of mounting the gun, rather than disengaging it when you think a shot may shortly present itself. Never, on a formal driven shoot, stand for the entire drive with the safety catch disengaged. Remember that, despite its name, the safety catch does not make the gun safe: only you can do that by unloading it. What the safety catch does is to lock the trigger mechanism. The action, meanwhile, remains cocked, ready to fire, and it may do so if it receives a jar or blow even if the safety is still 'on'.

Rarely are hammer guns used in the field today, but if you should use one, then cock the hammers only in the immediate expectation of a shot. If that shot, for whatever reason, is not taken, then, with the thumb firmly on the hammer and the barrels pointing in a safe direction, carefully pull the trigger and slowly return the hammer to the 'down' position.

Holding a shotgun at the ready, when awaiting the chance of a shot, barrels safely pointed at the sky.

WHEN IS IT SAFE TO TAKE A SHOT?

1. The general rule when shooting at a flying bird, is only to shoot when the bird is sufficiently high to ensure your shot cannot strike any person who might be standing close to you, remembering, of course, that if you are in hilly country there may be people who you cannot see who are standing well above you.
2. When shooting at a moving target on the ground, such as a running rabbit, it is all the more important to ensure that your line of fire is absolutely clear, and that there is nothing in the way that might obscure a lurking dog.
3. Always ensure that you have a clear view of your quarry before shooting, and that it is not partially hidden by vegetation.
4. Under no circumstances should you shoot through leaves or grass in the hope of hitting something that might be on the other side: you cannot possibly know what is on the other side in addition to your intended quarry.
5. If you are a guest on an organised shoot, you may well receive the instruction at the beginning to shoot 'no ground game'. Such a rule will have been imposed for safety's sake, to avoid any reason for low shots being taken.

Whether you are shooting alone or in company, always make sure before taking a shot that it is safe to do so. Remember that other shooters, beaters or dogs may be hidden behind trees, bushes or undergrowth. Therefore, do not attempt to take a shot against a backdrop of vegetation that may conceivably hide someone or something you do not intend to shoot. Ideally, you should only shoot at a bird when it is against a clear background of sky, and at an animal such as a rabbit or hare when it is on open ground and you can plainly see all that is round about it. However, in the shooting field ideal conditions rarely occur, and you must learn when it is safe to take a shot and when it is not.

All this may sound terribly daunting to the beginner, but it is not. In fact, it is a simple matter of looking carefully at your surroundings and noting the hazards and unsafe areas around you, then ensuring that if your quarry runs or flies towards those hazards, you do not shoot at it. With practice, you will gradually get used to noting subconsciously where it is safe for you to shoot. Remember that if you have the slightest doubt in your mind, there is absolutely no need for you to pull the trigger. None the worse will be thought of you for holding your fire, indeed, you will be marked out as a thoughtful shot who is conscientious about safety. It is far better that you do not shoot, even if it is at the only pigeon, pheasant or duck you have seen all day, than for you to take an unsafe shot. Once that trigger is pulled, no power on earth can stop those pellets in mid-air and bring them back again.

Crossing obstacles

One of the situations in which shooting accidents occur most frequently is when fences, hedges, ditches and other obstacles are being crossed. Very often, while out shooting you will have to negotiate an obstacle, and there are logical and recognised procedures for doing so, which vary according to whether you are alone or in the company of another person.

If you are with somebody else, both of you, as you approach the obstacle, should open your guns and unload them. Then one of you passes his gun, broken and unloaded, to the other person and proceeds to climb over the fence, through the hedge or across the ditch. When he gets to the other side and is on firm ground once more, the second shooter passes both guns, broken and unloaded, to the first shooter, before crossing the obstacle himself. Then the first shooter hands back his friend's gun, and the two can continue shooting.

When you are alone, the procedure must be different. Firstly, unload your gun, then pass it through the fence or obstacle, placing it securely on the far side where it will not fall or be damaged, then climb over or through the obstacle yourself. When you are on the far side, pick up the gun, check it, reload and continue shooting.

It might be tempting, when nobody else is about, to simply break your gun and, without removing the cartridges, clamber over a simple obstacle. Don't. Many is the shooter who has been found alone, dead or injured, beside a barbed wire fence or thorn hedge that was thought to be easy to cross without unloading. When passing through a gate that simply involves your undoing the catch and opening it, it is quite acceptable to break and unload your gun, then carry it through before reloading on the other side. The same goes for footbridges, steps and other simple obstacles that do not involve climbing or clambering.

Crossing a fence alone:

1. The shooter unloads his gun as he approaches the fence.
2. He puts down his gun securely on the far side of the fence, so that it will not fall over.
3. He climbs the fence.
4. He picks up his gun and reloads.
5. Continues.

Crossing a fence in company:

1. Both shooters unload as they approach the fence.
2. The first shooter passes his gun, open and breech first, to the second shooter.
3. He climbs the fence.
4. His gun is returned, open and breech first.
5. The first shooter takes the second shooter's gun.
6. The second shooter climbs the fence.
7. His gun is returned, open and breech first.
8. Both shooters reload their guns and continue.

performance steel shot cartridges will be marked with the 'fleur de lys' Special Steel Shot proof mark. Always check that the information printed on the cartridge box corresponds with that which is marked on the barrels of your gun.

LONDON	BIRMINGHAM	PROOF MARK
GP	BP	Provisional proof mark
–	B C P V	Definitive proof and view marks for black powder 1813–1904
–	BV BP	Definitive proof and view marks for black powder 1904–1955
GP	BP	Black powder proof mark 1955
NP	BP BV NP	Definitive nitro proof mark 1904–1955
NP	BNP	Definitive nitro proof mark 1955
GP	–	Definitive proof mark (on barrel pre-1955, on action since 1955)
R	R	Reproof mark used since 1925
GP	SP	Special proof mark used since 1925
STEEL SHOT		High performance steel shot
12		Nominal bore
65mm		Chamber length

HEARING PROTECTION

Regular exposure to loud noises causes progressive damage to the delicate mechanisms of the human ear. Moreover, that damage, once it has taken place, is irreversible, and no amount of medical attention can rectify it. The usual result of exposure to noise is a degree of deafness in one or both ears, and sufferers normally experience an inability to hear high-frequency sounds. A further feature of noise-induced deafness may be 'tinnitus', in which the sufferer hears a constant high-pitched ringing or whistling noise. Deafness and tinnitus are debilitating. They make it difficult to hear people speaking at normal conversational volume, especially when background noise levels are high.

Shooting exposes participants to repeated high levels of sharp or percussive noise, and everyone who takes part in the sport has a duty to themselves and their families to protect their hearing. Clay pigeon shooters, who may fire very large numbers of cartridges during the course of practice or competition, have long recognised the need to wear ear protection while they are shooting, but the acceptance of hearing protection has only more recently spread to live quarry shooters, which is why many older game shooters today suffer from 'gun deafness'.

Hearing protection comes in two basic forms. Tightly fitting earplugs prevent high frequency noise entering the ear canal, but do not protect the sensitive bones around the outside of the ear. 'Headphone' type ear defenders provide much better all-round protection. In order to overcome the drawback of wearers being unable to hear either their quarry or audible signals such as a horn or whistle, some ear defenders and custom-made earplugs are fitted with electronic systems that allow through ambient sounds such as normal conversation, but filter out loud noises.

Always wear ear protection whenever you go out shooting. If you do not do so, then you will be certain to regret it when, in time, your hearing fails.

5

CHAPTER 4

Shooting and the law

SHOOTING AND THE LAW

THE SPORT of shooting is regulated by a framework of laws that controls the possession of guns, defines the birds and animals that may be shot and regulates when, where and how we may shoot them. Other laws regulate the sale of game and control poaching. Although it is not necessary for the average shooter to have a complete knowledge of every aspect of shooting law, there are certain things that everyone who shoots must understand.

Shotgun certificates

In order to possess a shotgun, you will normally require a shotgun certificate issued by the police.

In Great Britain, firearms, including shotguns and air weapons, are controlled by the Firearms Act 1968 and a number of subsequent amending Acts. These state that, subject to certain exemptions, in order to possess a shotgun, a person must hold a shotgun certificate.

FORM 201 – 2017 - 1

APPLICATION FOR THE GRANT OR RENEWAL OF A FIREARM AND/OR SHOTGUN CERTIFICATE

PLEASE READ THE NOTES CAREFULLY (PAGES 12-15) BEFORE COMPLETING THE APPLICATION FORM

You may type your responses except where your signature is required. Otherwise, please use black ink and write in **BLOCK CAPITALS** throughout, except when signing. A continuation sheet is provided at page 6 for further information.

I am applying for (tick each box which applies)

- **Firearm certificate** ☐ Grant ☐ Renewal
- **Shotgun certificate** ☐ Grant ☐ Renewal

Do you wish to apply for a shotgun certificate which will expire at the same time as your firearm certificate? ☐ **Yes** ☐ **No**

PART A: Personal details.

1. Gender ☐ Male ☐ Female

2. Title ....

3. Surname ....

4. Forenames (state all) ....

5. If you have at any time used a name other than that given in answer to questions 3 and 4 please complete below:

Previous surname(s) ....

Previous forename(s) ....

6. Home address ....

....

....

a. Postcode ....

b. Home tel number ....

c. Mobile number ....

d. Home E-mail ....

Any previous home addresses in the last 5 years?

☐ Yes ☐ No (If yes please give details on page 2)

7. Height ....

8. Date of Birth ....

a. Place of birth ....

b. Nationality ....

9. Occupation ....

a. Work address ....

....

b. Postcode ....

c. Work tel number ....

d. Work E-mail ....

PART B: Personal health & medical declaration

If necessary, continue on page 6

Important: Read notes 4-12 before completion.

10. Have you ever been diagnosed with or treated for any of the medical conditions in note 5?

☐ Yes (Please provide details) ☐ No

....

11. Details of your GP or GP practice

a. Name ....

b. Address ....

....

....

c. Postcode ....

d. Tel number ....

e. E-mail ....

12. Details of all previous GP practices during the past 10 years (see note 12). Continue on page 6 if necessary.

a. Name ....

b. Address ....

....

c. Postcode ....

d. Tel number ....

e. E-mail ....

Are there any periods in the past 10 years when you have not been registered with a UK GP or have consulted medical practitioners other than at your GP practice?

☐ Yes (Please provide details on continuation page) ☐ No

I give the police permission to contact my GP and/or specialist to obtain factual details of any medical history in relation to my suitability to possess a firearm and/or shotgun. **This authority is valid for the life of the certificate(s).** I understand that my GP may share sensitive personal data with the police concerning my physical and mental health for the purpose of enabling the police to make a fully informed decision on my application or continued suitability, and I hereby consent to this processing of my personal data.

Applicant's name (please print)..........

Applicant's signature .... Date ....

The application form for the grant or renewal of a shotgun and/or firearm certificate may be obtained from the police or downloaded from the internet.

A shotgun certificate may be granted to a person who is normally resident in Great Britain, and if you wish to apply for one, then an application must be made to the police force in whose area you normally live. The application form (form 201) is available on the internet and may be downloaded from your police website or from the BASC site (www.basc.org.uk). This must be completed and returned together with the fee payable and one passport-style photograph of yourself. A digital image is required for an online application; a conventional photograph is required for a paper application.

A shotgun certificate may be granted to a person who is normally resident in Great Britain, and if you wish to apply for one, then an application must be made to the police force in whose area you normally live.

The applicant must supply details of a person who is resident in Great Britain, who has known them for at least two years and is of good character, and who is prepared to act as a referee. A referee may be of any background or occupation and should have had some reasonable degree of contact with the applicant over the past two years whether in a professional, business or social context. Members of the applicant's family or co-habiting partners may not act as a referee, and nor may a serving police officer or police employee, or a registered firearms dealer. It will be open for the police, if they so wish, to contact a referee in order to discuss with him or her the information that has been provided in the application, or any matter relating to it.

The applicant must also provide the name and address of their GP and details of any medical conditions that might adversely affect their ability to possess or use a gun safely. On receipt of the application, the police will contact the GP to check that the medical information that has been given is accurate and establish if there are any concerns that the GP may have about the applicant's ability safely to possess firearms.

The police will grant a certificate unless the applicant is debarred from possessing firearms by reason of a criminal record, or unless the police believe that he or she cannot be permitted to possess a shotgun without endangering the peace or the public safety. Any past convictions will be taken into account, but a person who has been sentenced to a term of imprisonment of three years or more is prohibited for life from possessing firearms. A person who has been sentenced to a term of imprisonment of from three months to three years is prohibited from possessing firearms for five years from his date of release. Particular rules apply to suspended sentences and secure training orders.

There is no need for an applicant to provide specific 'good reason' for requiring a particular shotgun as there is for a rifle. Taking part in sporting or competition shooting or vermin control are regarded as sufficient reasons for having a certificate.

A police Firearms Enquiry Officer will normally visit an applicant for a shotgun certificate at his or her home, by appointment. The purpose of this visit is for the police to check through the details of the application face-to-face and, if appropriate, to inspect the gun cabinet or storage facility where the shotgun will be kept, to see that it is suitable. The police will conduct a series of background checks on all applicants before issuing a shotgun certificate. They will operate according to the *Guide on Firearms Licensing Law*, which is published by the Home Office and which is regularly updated. That guide is available online by visiting the Home Office or BASC websites and it provides, at Chapter 11, a full explanation of the process of issuing a shotgun certificate.

A shotgun certificate is valid for five years from the date of grant or renewal, and contains the name, address and photograph of the holder, together with a list of the shotguns he or she possesses. Also indicated on the certificate is a series of conditions with which the holder must comply. First, they must sign the certificate in ink; second, they must within seven days inform the police of the theft or loss of any shotgun to which the certificate relates; third, they must without undue delay inform the police of any change of address; and fourth, they must store their guns securely.

At renewal, if it is not possible for the police to renew a shotgun certificate before the date on which it expires, then, provided that the application for renewal was made at least eight weeks before the date of expiry, the certificate will remain valid for an additional eight-week period.

Security of shotguns

It is the duty of the certificate holder to ensure that, so far as is reasonably practicable, access to his or her guns by an unauthorised person is prevented. This duty extends both to the home and to the many situations when guns are in use or in transit, and detailed information on the secure storage of guns may be found in the Home Office guide at Chapter 19. Most certificate holders store their shotguns in a steel cabinet, which must be securely fixed to the fabric of the building in which it is situated. When they are transported in vehicles, guns and ammunition should at all times be kept out of sight and preferably stored in a secure load-carrying compartment, such as a locked car boot. It is possible to buy devices that clamp or attach the gun to the bodywork of a vehicle. These may provide additional security and peace of mind. Ammunition should not be left together with a gun in an unattended vehicle.

Most certificate holders store their guns in a steel security cabinet.

It is advisable, when leaving a gun in an unattended car, to remove a working part, such as the fore-end of a shotgun, and conceal this separately or keep it with you.

When guns are kept in temporary accommodation, such as during a shooting trip away from home, then it is the certificate holder's responsibility to ensure that access by unauthorised persons is prevented. Many sporting hotels can offer storage in a gun cabinet, but it can be useful when staying away from home with a shotgun to carry with you a lockable security cord. When travelling with your gun, it is not a legal requirement for you to carry your shotgun certificate. However, a police officer may demand to see your certificate if he believes you to be in possession of a gun. While it is not unreasonable for you to wish to keep your original certificate in a safe place at home, it is sensible always to have a photocopy of it with you whenever you are out shooting. You must by law show your original certificate to the retailer each time you wish to buy cartridges.

Transfers

There are also rules regarding the transfer of shotguns between certificate holders. Whenever a shotgun is transferred from one certificate holder to another, whether it be sold, hired, given or lent, the transfer must be recorded on Table 2 of the recipient's certificate and both parties must inform the police firearms licensing department that issued their certificate within seven days of the transfer. The notification of transfer should include the date, the nature of the transfer, details of the gun – including the serial number – and details of both the transferor and transferee and their shotgun certificates. Such notification may be made in writing or electronically. It is not necessary, however, to complete Table 2 or notify the police if a shotgun is borrowed for a period of up to seventy-two hours. Nor is it necessary to notify transfers to a Registered Firearms Dealer, since these will be recorded in his dealer register.

Exemptions from the requirement to hold a certificate

There are certain circumstances in which a person may possess a shotgun without holding a shotgun certificate. These are as follows:

1. A person, such as a loader at a driven game shoot, may without holding a shotgun certificate have in his possession a shotgun and ammunition under instructions from another person, for use by that other person for sporting purposes only.
2. A person may, without holding a shotgun certificate, borrow a shotgun on private premises and have it in their possession on those premises provided that the person from whom the shotgun is borrowed is:

(a) aged eighteen or over

(b) the holder of a certificate in respect of the shotgun, and

(c) either:

(i) a person who has a right to allow others to enter the premises for the purposes of hunting animals or shooting game or vermin, *or*

(ii) a person who is authorised in writing by a person mentioned at (i) to lend the shotgun on the premises

The borrower may use the shotgun on the private premises to hunt animals or shoot game or vermin or shoot at artificial targets provided that, during the period for which the shotgun is borrowed, the borrower is in the presence of *either* the lender of the gun, *or* a person who, although not the lender, is a shotgun certificate holder aged eighteen or over and is a person described at (c) (i) or (ii) above. The term 'in the presence of' is generally taken to mean that the lender or other authorised person must be within sight or earshot of the person borrowing the gun.

A person may, without holding a shotgun certificate, borrow a gun on private premises under certain circumstances.

Where a person who has a right to allow others to enter the premises for the purposes of hunting animals or shooting game or vermin (for example the holder of the sporting rights) authorises in writing others to lend shotguns on the premises, then such written authorisation may be general in nature or it may specify individual persons to whom shotguns may be lent.

3. A person may, without holding a shotgun certificate, use a shotgun at a time and place approved for shooting at artificial targets by the Chief Officer of the police force for the area within which the place is situated. This allows the use of a gun at recognised shooting schools and clay shoots for which a special authority has been obtained from the police. The exemption only refers to artificial targets, and does not allow live quarry shooting by non-certificate holders.

4. The police may issue a temporary permit to allow a non-certificate holder to possess shotguns. Such a permit, known as a 'Section 7' Permit, is normally issued in special circumstances such as where the executor of a deceased person needs time in which to dispose of a shotgun that belonged to the deceased. A Section 7 Permit may also be issued when a certificate expires during the shotgun certificate renewal process because of delays by the police licensing department.

5. Visitors to Great Britain who wish to shoot there may obtain a Visitor's Permit. This is applied for by a host or sponsor who is resident in Great Britain from his local police firearms licensing department. If the visitor is an EU citizen, then the application must be accompanied by a copy of the visitor's current European Firearms Pass.

Shotguns and young people

In law, there is no set age below which persons may not hold a shotgun certificate. Any young person may potentially be granted a certificate provided that he or she is physically capable of handling a gun, though in practice, few certificates are granted to children under ten. Special provisions do apply to the possession and use of shotguns by young people. These are as follows:

1. A person under the age of fifteen may not have with him a shotgun unless he is under the direct supervision of a person of twenty one

or over, or unless the shotgun is in a securely fastened cover so that it cannot be fired.

2. A person aged between fifteen and eighteen may be given or lent a shotgun, and may use it without supervision. However, he may not buy or hire a shotgun or ammunition for it.

3. On reaching the age of eighteen, a person may buy or hire a shotgun and ammunition, provided that he has a shotgun certificate.

Remember that a young person requires a shotgun certificate unless covered by one of the exemptions listed on pages 79–81.

Shooting in public places

Special restrictions apply to the carrying of guns in public places. You may not carry a loaded shotgun in a public place – that is to say a place

A young person under fifteen must be supervised by a person of twenty one or over.

to which the public have, or are permitted to have, access – without lawful authority or reasonable excuse. Reasonable excuse might include having a loaded shotgun on a footpath running across the land over which you have the right to shoot. In any case, the responsibility of proving lawful authority or reasonable excuse lies with the person carrying the gun.

Particular care must be taken when you are shooting close to public roads. It is an offence under the Highways Act 1980, without lawful authority or reasonable excuse, to discharge any firearm within 50 feet of the centre of a highway if in consequence someone using the highway is injured, interrupted or endangered.

Whenever you are shooting, you must make absolutely certain that you have authority to be where you are. If you have no such authority, and have a gun with you, whether loaded or not, then you may be committing an armed trespass.

Armed trespass

While normally trespass is a civil offence, armed trespass is a criminal matter and carries with it a severe penalty. It is, therefore, wise to leave your gun behind – first making sure that it is secure – if for any reason you need to enter land over which you do not have the shooting rights, for example to retrieve a bird that has fallen beyond your boundary.

Sporting rights and poaching

In Britain, the right to take game and wildfowl usually goes with the ownership of the land. This right may be leased to another party, and very occasionally the shooting rights may be detached from the freehold of the land and owned separately. On areas of public land the shooting rights will sometimes be leased to an individual or a shooting club by the authority that manages that land, thus the Forestry Commission may lease shooting rights over its woods or the Crown Estate might lease shooting rights over a tidal estuary to a wildfowling club. It follows that even on most public land, there is no free or public right to shoot, the exception being on unregulated tidal foreshore in

Sporting rights are usually connected with the ownership of land.

Scotland. Although this may sound restrictive, in practice it has meant that game birds and many other wild species have remained far more abundant in Britain than in some other countries. The reason for this is that because a landowner or holder of sporting rights knows that he alone controls the shooting over his land, he has the incentive to preserve and protect the game there in the knowledge that someone else is not able to simply to walk in and lawfully shoot it.

This does, of course, mean that you must be very careful to ensure that before you go shooting you have the permission of the landowner or the holder of the sporting rights. If you do not, then you will be poaching and very likely committing an armed trespass into the bargain. All poaching may be dealt with severely by the courts.

Shooting wild birds

In Great Britain the legislation that regulates the shooting of wild birds, as distinct from game, is the Wildlife and Countryside Act 1981. This Act prescribes lists of birds that may be shot under certain circumstances and prohibits some methods of killing or taking birds.

Under the Wildlife and Countryside Act 1981, the following wild birds may be killed or taken by authorised persons during the open season:

coot
gadwall
goldeneye
golden plover
goose, *Canada*
goose, *greylag*
goose, *pink-footed*
goose, *white-fronted* *(in England and Wales only)*
mallard
moorhen
pintail
pochard
shoveler
snipe, *common*
teal
tufted duck
wigeon
woodcock

PROHIBITED METHODS OF SHOOTING WILD BIRDS

1. It is illegal to use any bow or crossbow.
2. It is illegal to use any explosive other than ammunition for a firearm.
3. It is illegal to use a semi-automatic shotgun capable of holding more than two rounds in the magazine. Note that this may not apply to 'pest' bird species listed on the general licences (page 87).
4. It is illegal to use a shotgun with an internal diameter at the muzzle exceeding (4.5cm) 1¾ inches.
5. It is illegal to use any device for illuminating a target or any sighting device for night shooting.
6. It is illegal to use any form of artificial light or any mirror or other dazzling device.
7. It is illegal to use as a decoy any sound recording.
8. It is illegal to use as a decoy any live animal or bird that is tethered, secured by braces or similar appliances, or which is blind, maimed or injured.
9. It is illegal to use any mechanically propelled vehicle, including a boat, in immediate pursuit of a bird or animal, for the purpose of killing it.

The seasons within which these birds may be taken are as follows:

WILD BIRD	SEASONS
woodcock *(England and Wales)*	1 October–31 January
woodcock *(Scotland)*	1 September–31 January
snipe	12 August–31 January
wild duck and geese *(inland)*	1 September–31 January
wild duck and geese *(below the high water mark of ordinary spring tides)*	1 September–20 February
coot, moorhen, golden plover	1 September–31 January

It is illegal to shoot these species on Christmas Day in Scotland, and on Sundays in Scotland and in certain English and Welsh counties (or former counties) and county boroughs, namely Anglesey, Brecknock, Caernarvon, Cardigan, Carmarthen, Cornwall, Denbigh, Devon, Doncaster, Glamorgan, Great Yarmouth County Borough, Isle of Ely, Leeds County Borough, Merioneth, Norfolk, Pembroke, Somerset and the North and West Ridings of Yorkshire.

In Northern Ireland there is no shooting on the foreshore after 31 January and all shooting at night, on Sundays and on Christmas Day is prohibited. Duck and goose species that may be shot are gadwall, goldeneye, mallard, pintail, pochard, scaup, shoveler, teal, tufted duck, wigeon, greylag goose, pink-footed goose, Canada goose. Wader species that may be shot are common snipe, jack snipe, golden plover, woodcock.

During periods of severe weather, the Secretary of State for the Environment may declare periods of special protection for wild birds, during which the shooting of wildfowl, snipe and woodcock is prohibited. A set of criteria based on observed meteorological readings has been agreed by the Government, the shooting organisations and the bird protection bodies for approving and implementing periods of special protection.

'Pest' birds

Certain other species of wild birds may be killed or taken by authorised persons at all times under general licences for the prevention of damage or disease, for health, public safety or conservation purposes. They may typically include:

crow
dove, *collared*
goose, *Canada*
goose, *Egyptian*
gull, *lesser black backed*
jackdaw
jay
magpie
parakeet, *monk*
parakeet, *ring-necked*
pigeon, *feral*
rook
woodpigeon

Licences may permit the use of cage traps, unrestricted semi-automatic firearms and other methods of killing and taking that are otherwise prohibited. Note that general licences are subject to annual review and are issued by the statutory nature conservation agencies for England, Wales, Scotland and Northern Ireland. Lists of species and permitted methods of killing and taking may vary between countries and from year to year. You should check on the relevant agency website or with BASC before shooting pest species.

Shooting game

Laws have regulated the killing or taking of game for hundreds of years, and some legal provision still in force in Great Britain date back to the Game Act 1831 and, in Scotland, the Game (Scotland) Act 1772. The law lists a number of birds that are normally regarded as 'game', and sets out the seasons when they may be taken. These are as follows:

GAME BIRD	SEASON
black grouse	20 August–10 December
pheasant	1 October–1 February
partridge	1 September–1 February
red grouse	12 August–10 December
ptarmigan	12 August–10 December

Game birds may not be shot at night, that is to say from one hour after sunset to one hour before sunrise. In England and Wales they may not be shot on Sundays or Christmas Day. In Scotland there is no prohibition on shooting game birds on Sunday or Christmas Day, but it is not customary to do so.

Shooting rabbits and hares

Rabbits and hares may be shot by authorised persons during the following open seasons:

RABBITS AND HARES	SEASON
brown hare *(England and Wales)*	no closed season *(but see below)*
brown hare *(Scotland)*	1 October–31 January
mountain hare *(Scotland)*	1 August–28/29 February
rabbit *(England, Wales and Scotland)*	no closed season *(but see below)*

The shooting of hares and rabbits is subject to a close season on moorland or unenclosed land in England, Wales and Scotland.

Moorland and unenclosed land does not include arable land or detached portions of land less than 25 acres that adjoin arable land. In England and Wales, occupiers and authorised persons may kill hares and rabbits between 1 September and 31 March. In Scotland, occupiers and authorised persons may kill hares and rabbits by shooting between 1 July and 31 March.

The Ground Game Act of 1880 gives occupiers of land the right to kill and take rabbits and hares. The original intention of this law was to ensure that tenant farmers had the right to protect their crops from damage. Rabbits and hares may be shot at night by the landowner or by persons authorised by him. An occupier of land, together with one other person authorised by him may also shoot rabbits and hares at night provided that if he does not hold the sporting rights to the land, then that person has the permission of the holder of those rights.

The sale of dead game and wild birds

Game may be sold throughout the year, except that dead hares may not be offered for sale between 1 March and 31 July. The supply of wild game (including hares, rabbits and wildfowl) for human consumption is controlled by food hygiene regulations. Game that is sold to an Approved Game Handling Establishment (AGHE) (game dealer) must be inspected by a trained hunter.

Those selling game for human consumption, other than to an AGHE, must be registered as a food business with the Local Authority. Certain wild birds may be sold dead between 1 September and 28 February. They are:

coot
golden plover
mallard
pintail
pochard
shoveler
snipe, *common*
teal
tufted duck
wigeon
woodcock

Woodpigeon may be sold dead at any time.
It is illegal to sell dead wild geese.

Shooting of mammalian pests

The following species may be controlled by legally approved methods, including shooting, at all times of the year throughout the UK:

cat, *feral*
fox
mice *(except hazel or common dormouse)*
mink
rabbit
rat, *brown*
squirrel, *grey*
stoat
weasel

Non-toxic shot

Restrictions apply to the use of lead shot for shooting waterfowl or for shooting over wetlands.

Restrictions apply to the use of lead shot for shooting ducks and geese or for shooting over wetlands. There are slight variations between the different countries of the UK.

In England and Wales, the use of lead shot is prohibited:

- on or over any area below the high water mark of ordinary spring tides
- on or over particular Sites of Special Scientific Interest that are important for waterfowl
- for the shooting of any duck, goose, moorhen or coot.

Thus, a prohibition on the use of lead is in place for all shooting over certain wetland areas whether it be for wildfowl, game or pest species. In addition, the species named within the legislation may not be shot using lead cartridges in any circumstances, even on a driven day over farmland.

In Scotland and Northern Ireland, the regulations take a habitat-based approach and prohibit the use of lead shot over wetlands as they are defined in international legislation. This includes marine and coastal wetlands; inland wetlands such as rivers, streams, ponds, pools and lakes; bogs or mires with visible standing water; artificial wetlands such as canals, reservoirs, gravel pits and flight ponds. Puddles and temporary pools that are present only after heavy rain are not included. If in doubt, it is best to assume that a wetland is covered by the regulations.

The legislation applies only to shotgun shooting, and does not prohibit the use of lead rifle bullets or airgun slugs.

CHAPTER 5

Game shooting

GAME SHOOTING

THE DRIVEN game shoot is the defining form of live quarry shooting associated with the UK and it is also the most popular. Each year, some 120,000 driven game shoots take place in this country, providing, in total, some 1.6 million 'Gun-days' of shooting activity, more than most other branches of quarry shooting put together. It is, of course, the form of shooting that features most strongly in the public imagination, thanks to all those TV costume dramas, and while in reality only a small minority of game shoots are associated with grand country houses and traditional estates, British game shooting has a worldwide reputation that draws thousands of shooters to this country each year from overseas.

It was a combination of factors that led, in the nineteenth century, to the development of driven game shooting in Britain. The perfection

Driven game shooting is one of the fastest growing and most popular branches of the sport.

of the breech-loading shotgun meant that sportsmen no longer had laboriously to load their guns from the muzzle after each shot, and so were able greatly to increase their rate of fire. This meant that they could successfully shoot at a steady stream of birds driven over them by a team of beaters. At the same time, the wealth created by the Industrial Revolution enabled landowners to engage vast teams of staff to establish large organised shoots. Finally, the system of land ownership that existed in Britain meant that game could be preserved for shooting over the entire area of large estates. Shooting became fashionable and landowners started to invest large sums of money in redesigning their estates to accommodate woods and spinneys that would improve the habitat for game and game shooting. The result was the creation of the great driven game shoots that had their high water mark in the Edwardian period before the First World War.

Over the last hundred years, access to driven shooting has grown exponentially. Improved technology has made the large-scale rearing of game birds far easier than was once the case, while new game management practices based on annual cover crops has enabled the development of driven shoots on farmland that does not benefit from traditional estate woods and coverts. Meanwhile, people have more disposable income and far more time to spend it than was once the case. No longer the prerogative of a small social elite, driven game shooting has become accessible throughout society. Syndicate shoots and commercial shoots that provide the opportunity for shooters to take up seasonal membership, rather as one might join a golf club, or that offer shooting by the day, have brought the sport within reach of a much wider circle of people. Moreover, the organised game shoot is no longer restricted to large country estates. Many farms now have quite sophisticated game shoots, spreading shooting opportunity far and wide across the countryside.

Improved technology has made the large-scale rearing of game birds far easier than was once the case.

What is game shooting?

A driven game shoot is simply one in which the shooters, or 'Guns', instead of flushing the birds themselves and shooting them as they fly away, wait at fixed stands or 'pegs', while a team of beaters drives the game towards them. If it is well organised over suitable terrain, a driven shoot will deliver fast, high-flying birds over the Guns, testing shooting skills to the extreme.

On the majority of driven shoots, the pheasant is by far the most important quarry species, indeed, it accounts for sixty-five per cent of all the game birds and wildfowl shot in the UK. A native of the Middle East, the pheasant was introduced to Britain some two thousand years ago. It is strong and flies very fast over short distances; it adapts well to a variety of habitats and can easily be reared and introduced to the wild. This is important, as driven game shooting requires a plentiful population of game if it is to be successful. Only a few shoots in areas of particularly favourable habitat can rely upon wild pheasants to form the bulk of their bag, and most need to rear game birds and release them into a suitably managed habitat.

Pheasants and partridges are the quarry most frequently shot by the driven game shooter.

The rearing and releasing of game, the management of the birds and their habitat, and the control of predators is the responsibility of the gamekeeper. Many estates and shoots employ full-time gamekeepers. Other gamekeepers work part-time or as amateurs. On the day of a shoot, it is the responsibility of the gamekeeper to marshal the other assistants whose job it is to ensure that the birds are flushed and directed over the Guns to present challenging, sporting shots. These include the beaters, who walk in line through the cover in order to move the birds forwards and flush them over the Guns, the stops, who are positioned at strategic points to prevent birds escaping out of the cover without flying over the Guns, and the pickers-up, who work their dogs behind the line of Guns in order to retrieve the shot game.

There are some 23,000 driven game shoots in the UK and they vary greatly in size. At one end of the scale are the very grand traditional estate shoots, in which a large staff is employed to make sure the day runs smoothly and at which guests often stand with the Guns to watch the shooting. Sometimes the Guns use a pair of shotguns and have next to them a loader, whose task it is to load the second shotgun while the first is in use. Shoots like this are important social occasions and a well-appointed lunch will invariably be laid on for the Guns and their guests, either midway through the day or after the shoot has finished. Shooting on this scale is expensive, and even those estates that run a private shoot, principally for the landowner to entertain his own personal guests, will very often let a number of days during the season to paying clients in order to recover a proportion of the costs involved. Other shoots, both large and not so large, are run on entirely commercial lines to return a profit to the estate or shoot operator.

Far more numerous are the modest shoots in which a group or syndicate of shooters clubs together in order to fund the cost of rearing and releasing the birds. The farmer or landowner over whose land the shoot operates may be a member of the syndicate, and very frequently the Guns themselves carry out the work involved in game management, perhaps with one of them who lives close to the shoot acting as amateur gamekeeper and ensuring that the birds are fed and watered, and that predators are kept under control.

Many shooters get their first taste of driven game shooting when they receive an invitation to attend a shoot as a guest of one of the regular Guns or syndicate members. Others may buy a day at one of the commercial shoots. In either case, a first day at driven game is very exciting but possibly also rather daunting. There is so much to think about and a great deal of preparation that must be undertaken, even before the day itself arrives.

Game shooting is accessible to both sexes and all ages.

A day's driven pheasant shooting

Whether it is a smart shoot or a modest one, the first thing that you must do upon receiving an invitation to a day's driven game shooting is to reply promptly, for to do otherwise is nothing less than discourteous to your host. Besides, the shoot organiser will be putting a great deal of effort into making the day a success, and he will want to know at the outset that he has a full team of Guns. Shoot days are often planned months in advance, so there is normally plenty of time to anticipate the big day and to think about what clothing and equipment you are going to take with you.

Most game shooters use a 12-bore gun, although many experienced shots today prefer the 20 or even 28-bore, and the smaller gauges are frequently the choice of women shooters and young shots.

First on the list will be your gun. A conventional double-barrelled shotgun is most appropriate, and it matters not whether it is of the traditional side-by-side or the over-and-under configuration. It is best to avoid semi-automatic shotguns since, as we have already seen, these cannot always be seen immediately to be safely unloaded when you are shooting in the company of other people. A gun slip will be necessary to cover your gun between drives.

Select the correct cartridges to go with your gun. A standard game load of between 28g (1oz) and 32g ($1^1/_{16}$oz) (for 12-bore guns) will be suitable, and shot size 6 or 7 will be best if you are expecting to shoot pheasants or partridges. Many shoots prefer the use of fibre-wadded cartridges, to prevent the problem of litter caused by plastic wads. You must also assess how many cartridges to take with you. Check with your host: he may be able to give you guidance on this point. But remember that it is better to have too many than too few. You can always bring them home again with you, and to run out of cartridges in the middle of a drive is the height of frustration, as well as being a discourtesy to your host.

Although a cartridge belt is an easy way of carrying your ammunition, most belts only hold 25 rounds, and on a driven day you can often expect to fire many more cartridges than that, so a cartridge bag is a better option for the game shooter, especially as he will normally be standing at a fixed point while he is shooting and so will not have both to carry his cartridge bag and shoot at the same time. Cartridge bags can be obtained with a variety of capacities. It is also possible to obtain a cartridge magazine that will carry several hundred cartridges. Left in the car, this will ensure a 'strategic reserve' of ammunition. If you do not have one, simply ensure that you have some spare boxes of cartridges with you. If wildfowl are permitted to be shot, then remember that you may need to shoot them with non-lead cartridges, so if necessary, ensure you have some of these with you.

Although working their own gundog is very important to many shooters, driven game shooting is the branch of the sport in which a dog is of least significance, as there are normally experienced pickers-up in attendance to ensure that all the game is retrieved. Some larger shoots actively discourage the Guns from bringing their own dogs. The smaller ones, where Guns are more likely to be responsible for retrieving their own birds, may well welcome dogs. In any case, check with your host before bringing a dog to a driven shoot, and do not even think about bringing it unless it is well trained and will not 'run-in' to retrieve birds as they fall, probably causing chaos and confusion in the process. As a beginner at game shooting you would be well advised to leave the dog behind. It will only be an

THE PHEASANT

Nobody can possibly mistake the pheasant for any other bird. The gaudy cock pheasant, with its speckled bronze body and wings, its iridescent green head and neck, its long tail and scarlet cheek patches, is one of the most striking of all birds in the British countryside. Its mate is smaller in size and considerably more dowdy, being a uniform mottled brown in colour.

Pheasants are indigenous to central and south Asia, and are only present in Europe as a result of deliberate introduction by man. It is generally believed that the species was brought to Britain by the Romans, and pheasant remains have been found in excavations dating from that period. Pheasants were well known in Britain before the Norman conquest and were established throughout England by the late fifteenth century. Today, pheasants are found widely throughout Great Britain, and are absent only from the Scottish highlands and the Welsh mountains. Mixed farmland interspersed with woodland is the pheasant's preferred habitat, and birds particularly enjoy woods with thick undergrowth to provide them with warmth and shelter. They nest on the ground, laying from seven to eighteen eggs, normally between late April and June. Rearing and releasing of pheasants for shooting takes place widely throughout the country, and there has been regular interbreeding between wild and reared populations.

extra worry on your mind during a day when you will want to focus all your concentration on your shooting. As you gain experience in the shooting field, then, if the shoot organiser is happy with your doing so, then by all means take your dog. However, if there is the slightest risk of it being 'unsteady' and of wanting to run-in to falling game or the sound of gunshots, then do not be embarrassed to make sure that it is firmly secured by a slip lead and a dog anchor.

Because of the social nature of game shooting, a great deal of attention has always been given to the correct form of dress. Although it is important to be properly turned out, both out of courtesy to your host and the other Guns and to ensure your own peace of mind, codes of dress for game shooting attract far more consideration than they actually deserve. A pair of breeks or plus-twos worn with woollen stockings and ankle boots or wellingtons for the bottom half, and a plain green or olive breathable waterproof shooting jacket over a comfortable sweater for the top half is more than adequate. With a collar and tie and a tweed cap or hat, you are there. An alternative option when the weather turns cold is a tweed field coat. Dressed this way, you will not be out of place on the smartest occasion.

On the day of the shoot, make sure that you arrive in good time. You will be greeted by your host and the shoot captain or organiser, who will provide you and the other Guns with a briefing on the rules of the shoot. He will stress the importance of safe shooting, and will tell you whether or not the shooting of ground game, that is to say rabbits and hares, is permitted. For safety's sake, many shoots prefer the Guns not to shoot ground game. Others prefer to preserve hares. Most gamekeepers will be only too delighted for you to shoot a fox if you get the chance, but do not attempt to do so unless you are explicitly told that you may, and even then, the chance must be both an absolutely safe one and very close indeed, for a shotgun loaded with bird shot is not really the most suitable weapon for foxes.

> The shoot captain explains any signals given to start and finish the drives. These are normally given on a horn or whistle. Unless you are given instructions to the contrary, you must not load your gun until you hear the signal to start the drive, and you must unload as soon as you hear the signal that it is over.

The shoot captain will also explain any signals given to start and finish the drives. These are normally given on a horn or whistle. Unless you are given instructions to the contrary, you must not load your gun until you hear the signal to start the drive, and you must unload as soon as you hear the signal that it is over. Perhaps you may be told that you are 'live on your peg'. This means that once you have arrived at your correct position for the drive, you may load and start shooting without any further signal.

You will then be invited to draw for your place, normally by selecting a numbered marker. The number you draw will give you the number of the peg at which you will stand for the first drive. It is usual for the Guns to move up two places between drives, so that the Gun who is at number 4 for the first drive becomes number 6 on the second and so on. This ensures that no one individual unfairly monopolises the best of the shooting all day. However, different shoots employ a range of procedures to move the Guns around in the line during the course of the day, and you will need to listen out for any instructions that you are given. At most shoots the drives will be pegged for between eight and ten Guns.

Check to see if you will be returning to your car at lunchtime or during the course of the day. If not, this is a cue for you to take any spare cartridges or clothing with you in the shoot vehicle. At this point, you and your fellow Guns will move off, perhaps in a 'Gun bus', a shoot trailer or in a convoy of 4×4 vehicles. On arrival at the first drive, do remember to avoid loud conversation as you are directed to your peg. Game can hear very well and will already be exiting the coverts in the wrong direction ahead of a chattering team of noisy Guns, much to the frustration of the gamekeeper and shoot organiser.

A tractor and trailer take the Guns to the next drive.

Let us imagine that it is a fine, crisp November morning, and your numbered peg is situated in the bottom of a shallow valley, where the grass is still white from the night's frost. In front of you is a dark covert with a cover crop in front of it, and behind you is more woodland. To the left and right you see your fellow Guns getting themselves ready to shoot. The first thing that you will do is to remove your cartridge bag and anything else that you are carrying and place it on the ground in front of you. It is a good idea to put a sufficient quantity of cartridges in your pockets so that you can reload quickly without having constantly to reach down during the drive. Remove your gun, broken, from its slip, check the barrels for obstructions, and if you have not been told that you are 'live on your peg', await the signal that the drive is about to start before loading your gun.

Now is the time to take your bearings. Check behind you to see if there are any pickers-up that you should be aware of. Similarly, look out for stops in the wood ahead, and make a mental note of your safe zones of fire. High birds coming over you or crossing in front of you may be shot at. You may also shoot at birds behind the line of Guns if it is safe to do so, remembering, of course, that if you wish to turn and take a shot behind then you must dismount the gun from your shoulder before turning with the barrels pointed directly upwards, remounting the gun only when you are facing a safe firing zone. Any low birds should be left: they only encourage dangerous shooting. You should also leave any bird that you can see will make a better driven shot for your neighbouring Gun than it will for you.

Low birds should be left: they only encourage dangerous shooting.

Before the drive starts, make sure you know exactly where your neighbouring Gun and any other personnel, such as pickers-up or stops, are standing.

A comfortable, natural stance makes it much easier to mount your gun and pick up your target.

It is galling to raise your gun at a high pheasant coming directly at you, only to see it crumple and fall at your feet following your neighbour's shot: nobody likes to stand next to a 'poacher', as a greedy shooter is sometimes called.

The whistle blows, and you slip two cartridges into the breech and close your gun. Far away, at the distant end of the covert, the beaters are starting to move, tapping with their sticks to nudge the pheasants forwards. It is some minutes before the birds start flushing, a time of tension as you stand alert, waiting, watching, listening. Then, further down the line there is the whirr of wings and the crowing of a cock pheasant, as the first bird soars high over the Guns. A spatter of shots and it sails serenely on, to be lost in the woods behind. Then a flush of birds, this time directly in front of you. Your neighbour takes one cleanly on your left, while a second bird seems to come directly for the gap between the two of you. Is it your bird or theirs? In the moment that it takes you to decide to shoot, the bird, a fine cock pheasant in full autumn plumage, has accelerated through the gap and your shot is yards behind its tail. You turn to see that, while you have been engaged

Right: When the weather conditions are ideal, with cloud cover and a fresh breeze, then game shooting is especially fast and exciting.

Below: On formal shoots there is often a mid-morning break for refreshments in the field.

with the cock on your left, a sneaky hen has come straight over your head. You miss that also. Such is driven game shooting.

All is not lost, though. You reload quickly to see another cock heading towards you. This time the gun is mounted smoothly, the swing is sweet and the shot sure. Your first driven pheasant tumbles to the ground ten yards behind you. All too quickly you hear the whistle that signals that it is time to unload. By now the beaters can be seen emerging from the last few metres of cover, and the drive is at an end. As you return your gun safely to its slip, you turn to see the pickers-up, stationed well back from the line of Guns, busy with their dogs, collecting the shot game.

Perhaps one of them approaches you to congratulate you on your shooting and to establish that all your birds have been retrieved. Then, with the memory of that first driven pheasant still fresh in your mind, and with a feeling of elation, you turn to join the other Guns and share with them success and failure as you move on to the next drive. Perhaps there will be refreshments and a light snack after the second drive, while on many organised driven shoots, lunch is arranged after the third or fourth drive. This can be anything from a formal affair indoors to a relaxing break in a barn where the Guns and beaters can chat about the morning's events over a mug of hot soup. You should make sure that you have checked with your host regarding the lunch arrangements, for on a less formal shoot you may be expected to bring your own lunch and vacuum flask. You may also be invited to have a drink with the other Guns, either at lunchtime or between drives. If you do so, then please take care. Alcohol and guns can be a dangerous mixture, and drink is the cause of many a rash or risky shot.

There is one other important point that must be checked with your host. On a formal shoot where a gamekeeper is employed, it is normal to offer him a tip at the end of the day in appreciation of the sport that he has provided as a result of his hard work throughout the year. Tipping can sometimes be a sensitive point, so it is best to enquire discreetly of your host beforehand whether or not it is expected, and if so, how much money is appropriate. The correct time to quietly offer the keeper his tip, together with a word of thanks for the day, is when he hands you the traditional brace of birds to take home with

Right: September sees the opening of the partridge season.

Below: The shot is plainly visible in this picture, taken just after the gun was fired. See how much forward allowance is being given to the partridge. The bird was cleanly killed.

you. Finally, when you get home, and after cleaning your gun and feeding the dog, do not forget to write a note of thanks to your host. This is one of those occasions when an old-fashioned handwritten card or letter means so much more than an email or text.

Partridges

So far, we have looked only at driven pheasant shooting, however, about a quarter of all the game birds shot in this country are partridges. Because the partridge shooting season opens a month before that for pheasants and because partridges achieve maturity relatively quickly, shoots are able to make an early start to their autumn programme by organising a number of partridge days during September and October before turning to the main pheasant coverts later in the year. In some cases, especially on arable estates that are not heavily wooded, partridges represent the principal quarry throughout the season.

The species that game shooters will encounter on virtually every partridge shoot is the red-legged or 'French' partridge. It is not a native species, but was introduced in the eighteenth century and has proved to be well suited to the sandy or chalky soils and relatively dry, warm climate of southern England and East Anglia. It is also particularly well suited to modern large-scale rearing and releasing systems. Partridges provide extremely fast, testing targets, and are a good match for the arable

THE RED-LEGGED PARTRIDGE

The red-legged or 'French' partridge is indigenous to southern Europe and was first successfully introduced into Suffolk in the late 1700s. In the wild it is largely confined to the southern and eastern half of Britain, although odd birds do turn up elsewhere from time to time.

It is a brightly coloured bird, with strongly barred flanks and a distinctive black and white eye stripe, and there is little differentiation in plumage between cock and hen. Eggs are laid in late April and May and they hatch at the beginning of June. The chicks are far less reliant on insect food than those of the grey partridge, and so the red-legged partridge has weathered the changes in farming patterns much better than its grey cousin. The red-legged partridge is a strong, fast flyer over short distances, and is particularly at home on the lighter, dryer soils of east and southeast England.

As a sporting quarry, the red-legged partridge is relatively easy to rear, and large numbers of birds are released each year for shooting.

THE GREY PARTRIDGE

The grey or 'English' partridge is a bird of traditional mixed open farmland, and one that has suffered considerably from the intensification of farming over the past forty years. As a result, numbers are in serious decline.

Small and dumpy in appearance, with grey upper plumage and a distinctive horseshoe-shaped chestnut marking on the breast, grey partridges remain together in family groups or coveys well into the winter. In January or February they pair up and in spring clutches of ten to twenty eggs are laid in a shallow and well camouflaged depression, normally beneath or beside a hedgerow. Hatching of the chicks occurs in early June, coinciding with the peak availability of the insect food on which the young birds rely. In the wild, chicks only switch to eating seeds and grain as they get older, and a ready availability of insect grubs is thus essential to their survival in the first few days of life. As a result, the widespread use of farm pesticides is particularly damaging to wild partridge populations.

The grey partridge is a strong and powerful flyer over short distances, and its ability to turn and climb rapidly as it bursts over a hedgerow made it one of our premier sporting birds. Some farms and estates maintain a shootable surplus of grey partridge through rearing and releasing, but a few favoured estates are still managed for wild grey partridges.

estates as they thrive in game cover crops such as maize, sorghum and millet, which are specifically planted for shooting by landowners or shoot managers. Birds are released into these cover crops during late summer and flushed out of them by the beating line on shoot days to fly over the Guns.

Very occasionally, it is possible to come across a covey of the native grey or 'English' partridge. These birds were once the mainstay of game shooting across much of England, but wild grey partridges rely on traditional patterns of farming that permit the presence of large numbers of insect larvae on which the chicks feed. As agriculture has modernised and land use has changed, so the grey partridge has declined, although there are still a tiny number of wild grey partridge shoots, where the farming system and the traditional gamekeeping skills of predator control and habitat management ensure that, in a good year, a shootable surplus of wild partridges is present. Where only a handful of grey partridges exist, Guns will often be asked not to shoot them.

For the novice game shot, and for many experienced ones too, distinguishing between a grey and a red-legged partridge as it hurtles towards you on a partridge drive is not easy. Briefly, greys tend to come forward in tightly bunched coveys, like swarms of bees, and they will often be heard chirruping to each other while on the wing. Redlegs do not usually vocalise on the wing and they tend to fly singly or in twos and threes rather than in family groups.

Grouse

Pheasants and partridges form the backbone of the conventional low ground game shoot. There is, however, a very different form of game shooting which is to be found on the heather moors of northern England, Scotland, and a few parts of Wales. Grouse shooting is reckoned by many to be the finest of all forms of game shooting. Not only is the red grouse an exceptionally fast and agile bird, which offers some of the most difficult of all shooting, but it also has its home in the most glorious upland countryside. The combination of sporting shooting and magnificent scenery, once experienced, is never forgotten, and draws grouse shooters back to the moors year after year.

Driven grouse shooting

The red grouse is unique to the British Isles, and since it cannot be artificially reared, grouse shooting relies entirely upon the creation of suitable habitat in which the birds can breed and flourish, and upon the control of parasites and of predators such as foxes. This time-consuming and laborious habitat management and predator control work is the job of the moorland gamekeeper.

Where the moor is actively managed to ensure a high population of grouse, driven shooting is normally practised.

THE RED GROUSE

Native only to Britain, the red grouse is a sub-species of the willow grouse, which inhabits the northern regions of both America and Eurasia. The red grouse lives on high ground, especially heather moorland, in Scotland, northern England and Wales. A few red grouse may be found in Ireland.

Compact and energetic, the red grouse is a skilled and powerful flyer, and quite distinctive in its dark rufous plumage, which blends perfectly with the colour of the heather. It is recognised worldwide as a premier sporting bird, and attracts many shooters to Britain from overseas to sample the unique shooting that it provides.

Red grouse cannot be reared, and proper habitat management is therefore essential if numbers are to be maintained. Grouse are very territorial, and like to nest in the security of deep old heather with younger heather nearby for feeding. The hen lays a clutch of six to twelve eggs in a heather-lined depression in the ground between late April and May, and the young chicks mature rapidly. Breeding success is often at the mercy of weather conditions; however, the scourge of parasitic worm infestation has been tackled in recent years through the widespread use of medicated grit and the sharp fluctuation in grouse populations is far less than it once was.

Until the turn of the present century, grouse populations followed a cycle of boom and bust, with very successful years that were followed by years with poor reproductive success. The cause of this was a complex network of factors that centred around a parasitic nematode, the strongyle worm. However, new management practices, coupled with the use of anthelmintic medicines applied to the grit that grouse require in order to grind up and digest the heather shoots on which they feed, have effectively broken the nematode's grip and enabled moors to maintain a high, stable population. In consequence, moorland estates have been able to offer more consistent shooting programmes that have brought

Above: Driven grouse shooting. This grouse butt has been beautifully built of turf and stone. Note the safety sticks at its corners to prevent the shooter from accidentally swinging through the line

Right: Grouse provide some of the most exciting game shooting in Britain.

considerable economic benefits to the uplands of northern England and parts of Scotland.

As with driven pheasant shooting, a driven grouse day employs teams of beaters to drive the birds towards the Guns. There, however, the similarity ends. Grouse drives take place across wide, open moorland, and the beaters often have to walk many miles in order to move the coveys forwards and ensure that they end up flying over the Guns. Their job is an arduous one, especially when the weather is very hot or when the rain lashes down later in the year. When shooting pheasants, the Guns are generally positioned in the open. Grouse shooters, however, are normally concealed in specially constructed 'butts'. These may either be temporary screens made of wood or permanent structures, often beautifully built of turf and stone. Because of the long time it can take the beaters to drive the grouse towards the butts, grouse shooters are often thankful for the shelter that a well-built butt provides.

If you are lucky enough to be invited to shoot driven grouse, then there are a number of additional points that you should bear in mind. Grouse travel very fast indeed when they are flying towards you in a drive. But they also fly very low, hugging the contours of the ground like surface-skimming missiles, and they can be upon you before you have time to think. Rather like partridges, they frequently cross the line of butts in coveys and later in the autumn these coveys often amalgamate into large packs. When shooting it is therefore essential that you select your bird well in front and shoot early. If you leave a driven grouse too long before shooting, it will almost certainly have crossed the butts and be out of range before you have had time to bring your gun to bear.

The sheer speed and agility of the grouse makes driven grouse shooting very exciting.

The sheer speed and agility of the grouse makes driven grouse shooting very exciting indeed, although the periods of excitement may be interspersed with long spells of waiting while the beaters bring the drive in towards the butts. Excitement, however, can lead to lapses in safety. Always remember that you may only take birds that are in front, behind, or well up above your butt. Never on any account shoot down the line of the butts at a low flying target, for in doing so you

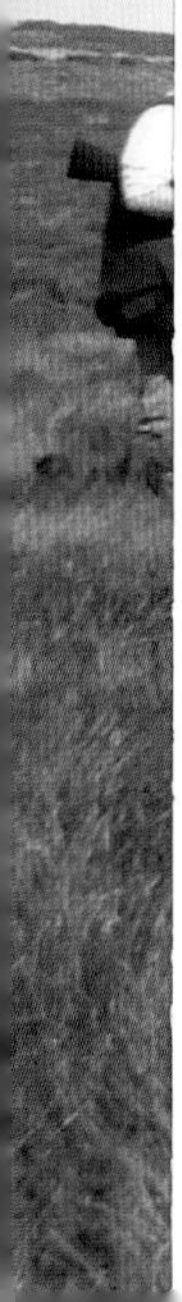

of stout lace-up leather boots with good ankle support which will keep your feet comfortable all day over rough terrain. A pair of gaiters worn over them will keep the heather seeds from collecting in your boots. On a warm August day, all that may be required for your top half is a shooting vest over a short sleeved shirt, but a sweater or jacket may be more sensible if the weather is cooler. Remember that the temperature is likely to be lower when you are high up on the moor, and also that anything you need during the day, whether it be waterproof clothing, food or spare cartridges, you may well have to carry with you if it cannot be left at some strategic point in a vehicle. It is too late, when you are 600 metres up a Scottish mountain and it is coming on to rain, to decide that you needed that waterproof coat you left back in the Land Rover after all.

When walking-up grouse, make sure that you stay in line and follow the instructions of the gamekeeper or shoot captain.

When walking-up grouse, make sure that you stay in line and follow the instructions of the gamekeeper or shoot captain. In rough country it is sometimes all too easy to lose touch with the Guns or walkers on either side of you, so make sure you are aware at all times where it is safe to shoot. On steep slopes, the person next to you may be several metres higher than you are, so take extra care when shooting at birds that fly through the line: a shot that, if taken on flat ground would be at an elevation that is perfectly safe, when translated onto a steeply sloping grouse moor might well endanger a Gun or walker above you in the line.

On a walked-up day, you are effectively combing in turn each section of the moor and hoping, perhaps with the aid of close-hunting dogs like spaniels, to flush whatever birds are there. There is, however, a third method of shooting grouse in which a pointing dog is used to find the birds and so allow one or two Guns to get into position for a shot before they are flushed. 'Dogging the moors' with pointers or setters is the oldest form of grouse shooting and is a very specialised form of sport. A pointing dog such as an English pointer or setter is used to quarter over the moor in an attempt to catch the scent of a hidden covey. The dog may range far in front of the Guns, but when it scents birds ahead it halts and stands rigidly, 'pointing' at them. The Guns then hurry forward to where the dog is standing, upon which the handler allows his dog to flush the grouse, hopefully giving the Guns the chance of a shot. If the pointer is not trained to retrieve, then a specialist retriever will be used to pick up the fallen grouse. The pickings are usually slim, and you should never expect more than a few brace of grouse on a day over pointers, but if you enjoy watching working dogs going about the task for which they have been bred and trained, then you should never turn down the opportunity of a day's dogging for grouse.

Other grouse species

The red grouse is, from the shooter's point of view, by far the most important of the grouse species to be found in the British Isles. There are, however, two other related quarry species which are occasionally encountered.

Black grouse.

The black grouse is found on the moorland edges, often amongst scattered groups of birch or rowan trees. It is larger than the red grouse and its strong, fast flight is less aerobatic than that of its red cousin. Black grouse were once found on moors and heaths all over southern England, but they are today in serious decline, probably due to changes in habitat, and are now to be found only in the uplands. On many shoots where they occur, they are voluntarily protected.

Ptarmigan.

Ptarmigan are birds of the tundra, and are the only British species of grouse to change colour with the seasons, turning white as winter approaches to match the snowy landscape of their natural habitat. They live on rocky mountain tops in the Scottish highlands, normally at altitudes in excess of 800 metres. Ptarmigan shooting is a specialised form of sport that involves a great deal of arduous climbing.

CHAPTER 6

Rough shooting

ROUGH SHOOTING

THERE is no quick and easy way to define the term 'rough shooting', despite the fact that it encompasses a large proportion of the sporting shooting carried out in Britain today. Perhaps the simplest way to describe the sport of the rough shooter is informal shooting that takes place over land not managed by a gamekeeper and where game is not deliberately reared and released or driven over the Guns. Rough shooting involves the pursuit of a wide variety of different birds and animals, from game birds such as the pheasant, to wild ducks, woodpigeons, rabbits, hares and waders such as woodcock and snipe. Variety in the bag is matched by the variety of the countryside in which the rough shooter enjoys his sport. Farmland, woods, hedgerows, heaths, ponds, rivers, lakes, even derelict industrial land all provide exciting opportunities for rough shooting, giving many thousands of shooters the chance to hunt game, often at very little cost.

An informal day's rough shooting – a chance to relax in good company.

Clothing and equipment

Because it is an informal sport, the emphasis when choosing equipment and clothing for rough shooting should be on the practical. Most shooters rely on a single versatile 70mm ($2\frac{3}{4}$ inches) chambered 12-bore shotgun. This is capable of handling a variety of cartridges to suit the quarry most likely to be encountered. A 30g ($1\frac{1}{16}$oz) or 32g ($1\frac{1}{8}$oz) game load of number 6 or 7 shot is sufficient to deal with most winged game, but if the main quarry is rabbits or hares, number 5 shot may be more suitable. If there is the possibility of getting a shot at a wild duck or goose, then it is worth keeping a couple of non-lead cartridges in your top pocket.

The rough shooter generally has to walk in search of his quarry, so everything he needs to take with him must be carried, from cartridges to sandwiches. A cartridge belt is a very practical way of carrying ammunition, and it is a good idea to select one that has closed ends to the loops. This ensures that the cartridges are kept as clean and dry as possible. A good, stout game bag is very useful. The best types have a net front for carrying game so that it can cool quickly, and a waterproof inner compartment. Alternatively, you may choose to carry one or two birds in a 'poacher's pocket' in your coat or on a strap suspended from your belt. Remember, though, that everything you carry must be comfortable enough for you to be able, while carrying it, to mount and swing your gun smoothly and shoot without effort should a pheasant suddenly rise or a rabbit bolt from the brambles in front of you.

The rough shooter generally has to walk in search of his quarry, so everything he needs to take with him must be carried, from cartridges to sandwiches.

In most situations to be encountered by the rough shooter during a British winter, a pair of wellington boots is ideal, preferably with comfortable socks inside to prevent chafing. A practical pair of breeks or trousers in cord or moleskin can be complemented in wet weather by waterproof overtrousers or leggings with the bottoms worn outside your wellingtons. Overtrousers are especially useful when you are expecting to walk through thick, wet cover such as kale or sugar beet. The choice of shooting jackets is very wide indeed, but you should ensure that whatever you select is suitably windproof and has a waterproof breathable membrane or liner. It should zip or fasten up around the neck and have adequate cuff fastenings to keep out the rain, and it should also be quiet in every sense of the word: with fabric soft enough not to rustle and crackle as you walk through heavy vegetation and in a colour or pattern that blends into the countryside. Large side pockets are useful for cartridges if you are not wearing a belt, and a lined game pocket will accommodate a bird or two if you are successful or your lunch if you are not. Whatever coat you choose, however, make sure that it is sufficiently roomy for you to mount and swing your gun easily. Tight clothing is constricting and uncomfortable.

A hat is important both to keep your head warm in winter and to ensure that your face is better hidden from the birds that you are trying to hunt. Finally, a pair of gloves or mittens can, on a cold day, make all the difference between comfort and misery. Cold hands make shooting difficult. They can even make it hazardous if fast, positive contact with triggers and safety catch is lost.

The lone rough shooter can hunt at his own pace and in his own way.

Hedgerow hunting

Perhaps the most popular form of rough shooting is simply walking-up hedgerows and ditches in search of game, usually with the help of a gundog. Its enjoyment comes from the fact that the shooter can hunt at his own pace and in his own way, taking pleasure in the sights and sounds of the countryside and using his own skills and those of his dog to create the chance of a shot. On a hedgerow hunting expedition the size of the bag is of little relevance. To the lone rough shooter, a single pheasant or pigeon stalked, flushed and killed after a successful shot is worth a dozen or more birds shot on a busy day's driven game shooting.

Tactics for hedgerow hunting may vary, but one thing always remains constant, and that is the need for stealth, silence and careful observation. By using the natural cover of overhanging trees or undulations in the ground it is often possible to get close enough to a sitting rabbit or roosting pigeon to ensure that you get a shot the moment it dashes for cover or flaps frantically from its perch.

While pigeons will flush and rabbits will readily bolt at the sight of a human hunter, it is much harder to flush game birds such as pheasants or woodcock if you do not have a dog, and the relationship between the rough shooter and his gundog – particularly one he has trained – is something very special indeed. Learn to understand every message your dog is trying to tell you and be on the spot the moment it feathers its tail and dives excitedly into cover, otherwise you could well miss the chance of a shot. Of course, it is important to ensure that your dog hunts close to you. If it does not, then it may put up any amount of game, but the birds and beasts that it disturbs will more than likely be out of range. An endless succession of pheasants rising forty yards away, ahead of an uncontrollable dog, is one of the most frustrating things that the rough shooter can experience.

A good dog will tell his master when there is game about or, conversely, when there is no point in hunting out that bramble bush any further.

Shooting with a companion

If there is no dog to flush them, game birds will frequently run ahead of the shooter as he walks along a hedge or ditch. Even if they do get themselves airborne, they can be extremely cunning, usually making sure that they rise on the opposite side of the hedge from the shooter. That is one of the reasons why it is a good plan to go shooting with a companion. It is far easier for two Guns to cover every possible angle of escape for a pheasant than it is for a lone shooter to do so, and by ensuring that one Gun walks on each side of the hedgerow, then no matter which way the bird flushes, one of you should have it covered.

Shooting with a companion, however, means that you must always be aware of your partner's location. Often, when rough shooting you will be working around thick patches of cover such as trees or bushes, which will hide one shooter from another. On top of this, it is quite likely that you will both be moving. The golden rule, therefore, is never to shoot where you cannot see that it is safe to do so. Do not shoot through hedges or undergrowth or take a shot at a low bird flying in front of cover. You just never know what may be behind it. Ground game poses special risks since, of necessity, shooting at it involves taking shots at ground level. Never shoot at ground game unless you can clearly see all the ground around it.

It is far better to let a pheasant, pigeon or rabbit go than to take a shot that, even though it might technically be safe, will, nevertheless, frighten or alarm a passer-by.

It is all the more important to strictly observe the rules when you are shooting close to a public road or footpath. A passer-by, unaware that shooting is taking place nearby, can easily be alarmed or upset at the sound of shooting or at spent pellets falling around him. To upset a member of the public will probably colour his or her view of shooters for many years to come, and may even do permanent damage to the reputation of shooting.

Rabbit shooting

The rabbit has long been one of the most important quarry species for the rough shooter. Rabbits are a serious agricultural pest because of the damage they do to growing crops. Although they were almost wiped out in the 1950s when the disease myxomatosis was deliberately introduced to control their numbers, many rabbits have now become immune to the disease and in recent years the population has greatly increased once again. Rabbits may be shot at all times of the year, and a good time to ambush them is on warm summer evenings when they are feeding some distance away from their warren. The specialist rabbit shooter may well use ferrets to flush the rabbits from their burrows. In this case, it is likely that those burrows that cannot be covered effectively with a gun will have nets placed across them to catch the rabbits as they try to escape. Shooting when ferrets are working underground requires extra care, as a ferret may easily follow a rabbit out of the burrow as it bolts.

Shooting rabbits by night from the back of a vehicle has become very popular, and is an extremely effective method of control. However, it can be hazardous if not carried out with great care. If you are planning to shoot from a vehicle, make sure that you have a firm, stable shooting position. Wear warm, comfortable clothing, and footwear that will give you a firm grip when you start shooting. Discuss with the driver beforehand how he intends to cover the ground, and shoot only those targets that are fully illuminated by the vehicle's headlights or by a separate lamp. Never shoot from a fast-moving vehicle. It is a good idea to inform the police if you are likely to be shooting after dark, especially if it is within earshot of nearby houses. A call to the non-emergency 101 line with the time and location of where you will be shooting will help to prevent any confusion should a local resident, unaware that you are carrying out rabbit control, report hearing shots close by at night.

Snipe and woodcock

Almost every type of countryside has shooting potential.

If the ground over which you are shooting has an area of wet or boggy land, particularly one where cattle have been grazing, then you might be lucky enough to get a shot at snipe. These small wading birds have long been prized by shooters, and present a particularly testing target as they zig-zag away when flushed. Snipe prefer wet grassland with plenty of tussocky sedge, rushes and standing water. They are easily alarmed, and should therefore be walked-up with stealth. Try to approach potential snipe ground quietly and with the wind at your back. This will mean that the birds will have to take off towards you before they turn and fly away. Although snipe breed throughout Britain, the snipe population is greatly augmented in winter by migrant birds arriving from Scandinavia and Iceland. However, because they need soft ground in order to feed for tiny invertebrates with their long, flexible bills, a prolonged frost will cause them to move south or west in search of milder conditions.

The woodcock is traditionally regarded as a game bird and is highly prized by game shooters when it is flushed by the beaters on a pheasant drive. Both snipe and woodcock are very good to eat.

Another migratory bird that is often encountered by the rough shooter is the woodcock. Although technically a wader, it does not inhabit marshy ground like other wading birds. Instead, it lives in mixed woodland and dense thickets interspersed with pasture, where it feeds on earthworms. There are shooting estates that specialise in woodcock shooting. These are mostly in the southwest of England and west Wales where large numbers of migrant woodcock regularly spend the winter.

Many woods will hold a few woodcock, however. Often, they can be found in the densest part of the wood where there are a few evergreen shrubs such as holly or rhododendron bushes. When disturbed, they will flit silently through the branches, and you will need to be very quick in order to get a clear shot. If you are shooting with a companion, then it is a good idea to work through any likely woodcock cover together, one walking on each side to maximise the chance of someone getting a shot should a woodcock be there.

The walked-up shoot

Although most rough shooters hunt alone or with a single companion, many rough shoots are more organised, bringing together a number of guns for a day's walked-up shooting. Farms that do not form part of a shooting estate very frequently organise a few days of walked-up shooting during the season, and the opportunity to join a group of other shooters for a friendly day's sport in the countryside is not to be missed. A walked-up shoot is far less formal than a driven game shoot, but it can, nevertheless, mean a great deal of organisation and planning on the part of the host, and can often involve a considerable number of people. So if you accept an invitation for a day's walked-up shooting, make sure you return your host's courtesy by turning up at the meeting point on time, and with everything you need.

Imagine that you have become friendly with a local farmer and, knowing that you are interested in shooting, he has invited you to one of the regular shoots that he holds on his land for your first day's walked-up pheasant shooting. Before the big day you will have got ready all your shooting gear, making sure that everything is in good repair and that it will not let you down when you are out in the field. The equipment required is exactly the same as you would need for any other day's rough shooting, but remember that you might be taking many more shots than you would on a hedgerow ramble, so put an extra box of cartridges into the car. Also, if you are walking through leafy crops like sugar beet or kale, then you are likely to get very wet if you do not wear a pair of waterproof overtrousers or leggings. And don't forget your game bag. You may well have to carry what you shoot for some considerable distance.

At the farmyard where the shoot is meeting, there is a buzz of activity. Your host introduces you to the other Guns, and very soon

Guns and beaters walk-up a field of sugar beet. Rough shooting is much less formal than driven game shooting.

you are swapping stories and joking with them. Meanwhile, your dog is doing exactly the same, for while on a formal driven shoot a dog may be an unnecessary distraction, when you are walking-up game, a good team of dogs is essential. Don't hesitate to take yours with you, provided of course that it is sufficiently well trained not to spoil the shooting for you or the other Guns.

Once you have got your coat, boots and overtrousers on, and having left your spare cartridges in the car after checking that you will be coming back to the farmyard at lunchtime, you climb aboard a farm trailer with the other Guns and dogs or maybe squeeze into the back of a 4×4 for the journey to the first drive, which is to be through a large field of sugar beet. On leaving the vehicle you remove your gun from its slip, break it, and keep it open and unloaded until the drive actually starts. This way, everybody can see, even from a distance, that your gun is safe. You are asked by your host to line out along the edge of the field. Because it is a big day, there are a number of beaters and dog handlers in the line as well as the Guns, so your host makes sure that the walkers and dog handlers are evenly spread along the line, alternating with the Guns. Then, at a given signal, you load and close your gun, remembering to keep the muzzles pointed at the ground in front of you, and the drive commences.

If for any reason somebody has to stop, perhaps to retrieve a bird that has fallen behind the line, then the whole line must stop together. Only when everybody is ready can the line start moving once more.

As you walk, carry your gun in one of the accepted ways – either over your forearm, muzzles pointing down or, grasping the fore-end with one hand and the grip of the stock with the other, with muzzles pointing safely upwards. You are concentrating, of course, on keeping your footing as you walk through the thick sugar beet, and looking hard at the cover in front of you, in the hope that very soon a pheasant might flush from it and give you your first chance of the day. But you must also keep a close watch on your neighbours to the left and right in order that the line is kept straight. A straight line of Guns is essential in walked-up shooting. If one individual forges ahead of the line or drops behind it, then he immediately reduces the safe angles of fire for those Guns on either side of him. This is annoying for the other Guns and indeed positively dangerous.

Perhaps the line of Guns has to change direction, and you are asked to pivot on the left- or right-hand Gun. Again, this manoeuvre must be carried out while keeping the line as straight as possible, the outermost Gun performing an arc around the one at the other end of the line, who remains stationary until the manoeuvre is completed.

If you have a dog with you, then there will be plenty to occupy your mind as you bash through the sugar beet. Ideally, the dog should quarter the ground in front of you, hunting back and forth at a distance of twenty metres or so from the advancing line of Guns. In this way, the maximum amount of cover can be hunted for game, and there is far less chance of any bird escaping by sitting tight and waiting for the Guns to walk past it. If, however, you are not sure of your dog's ability to quarter at close range, then it is better to keep it walking to heel unless it is actually retrieving. A dog that races forward out of control and flushes game 40 metres ahead of the line will spoil the drive for you and everyone else.

Your dog should quarter the ground in front of you, hunting back and forth at a distance of 20 metres or so from the advancing line of Guns.

When, with a flurry of wings a pheasant startles you by exploding from the beet just ahead, take the shot in as calm and measured a way as you can. Most walked-up birds will be going-away shots at a rapidly accelerating target. A first barrel fumbled through alarm or excitement may not leave you sufficient time to recover the situation with your second shot. Much better to let the bird get well into the air, steady yourself and read its line before pulling the trigger. Remember also that your pheasant is likely to be climbing fast. Blot it out with your barrels and keep your shot over it as it rises, and you will see it tumble satisfactorily into the beet ahead of you. The majority of going-away pheasants are missed underneath.

Stand and walk

A variation on the conventional walked-up day is that in which the Guns take it in turns to stand and walk. At the start of the day you will split into two equal teams. One team will act as standing Guns at one end of a piece of cover, while the other will line out at the opposite

Bags are usually not large, but every bird is well earned.

Rough shooting offers companionship plus plenty of healthy exercise.

end in the conventional manner and walk it up towards them. At the next drive the teams will change places and those who have just done the walking will take their turn as standing Guns. Usually, the stands are informally arranged, and there are no numbered pegs to go to, which, of course, makes it all the more important to listen closely to the instructions that you are given before the beginning of the drive by the shoot organiser.

There are a couple of other points that need to be borne in mind when you are shooting in this manner. As a walking Gun you will usually be asked to leave any birds that fly forwards, so that these can be dealt with by the standing Guns in front of you, but you may well be invited to shoot at those that endeavour to break out of the sides of the drive, those that flush behind the line or those that curl back over your head in an effort to escape. Even so, you must remember that you are walking towards a line of Guns, possibly concealed behind a hedge, and it is therefore dangerous to take any low shot in front of you. Likewise, if you are standing, ensure that any bird you shoot at is high enough to avoid endangering the walkers as they make their way towards you. If it is too low, then leave it for another day.

CHAPTER 7

Wildfowling

WILDFOWLING

DUCKS and geese offer some of the most exciting shooting in Britain. Apart from a limited number of mallard that are reared and released by shooting estates, almost all the birds that the shooter might see as he walks out onto the marsh or waits beside the river or flight pond are absolutely wild. To hunt such a wary, keen-eyed and intelligent quarry successfully means understanding its behaviour and being willing to learn the fieldcraft necessary to enable you to get close to it or to bring it close to you. Above all, it requires an enthusiasm to seek out the wild places where ducks and geese gather, and to do so at times of day or night and in weather conditions that would make most people want to be back at home watching the TV or tucked up in bed.

It is this connection between ducks and geese – known collectively as 'wildfowl' – and the wild and lonely marshes, estuaries, rivers, lakes and fens, that injects wildfowling with a special magic that many shooters find irresistible. It is no accident that the sport has captivated generations of writers and artists.

The opportunity to hunt in wild places at dawn or dusk is part of the thrill of wildfowling.

Wildfowl may be hunted either inland, over rivers, flight ponds and freshwater marshes, or below the high tide mark across salt marshes and estuaries. Experienced wildfowl shooters will sometimes say that only coastal duck and goose shooting can properly be described as 'wildfowling', and that anything else is simply either duck or goose shooting. It is true that real wildfowling requires great stamina and determination, and that to be a wildfowler you have to be prepared to face foul weather and difficult, even dangerous terrain, often at highly antisocial hours of the day and night. However, mastery of wildfowling skills and willingness to overcome wind, rain and cold is just as important on the bleak marshes above the sea wall as it is on the foreshore, and although it is true to say that salt water and the ebb and flow of the tide add a dash of spice to wildfowling, it is unfair to brand inland shooting as a lesser sport. What distinguishes all wildfowling from other forms of sport with the shotgun is the fact that most of the ducks and geese shot by wildfowlers in Britain are migratory birds that breed in northern Scandinavia, Iceland and Arctic Russia and that may travel thousands of miles each autumn to their traditional wintering grounds. In the depths of winter, when the freshwater ponds and rivers are frozen and only the salt water remains open to wildfowl, vast numbers of migratory ducks, geese and waders may pack into the estuaries of Britain. The fact that migratory wildfowl are a resource that we share with other countries means that we have an international responsibility to care for and conserve the natural habitat on which they depend. That is why the most important wildfowl sites are protected under international law. Wildfowlers take

Wildfowling on inland marshes is a challenging sport.

> The most important wildfowl sites are protected under international law. Wildfowlers take their responsibility to conservation very seriously indeed.

Shooting the tidal foreshore is often regarded as the cream of wildfowling.

their responsibility to conservation very seriously indeed, and there are long established links between the sport and the conservation movement.

Wildfowl identification

A knowledge and understanding of wildfowl and their habits is essential to success in wildfowling, whether above or below the sea wall. The first priority for the newcomer to wildfowling is to be able to recognise the quarry species he is likely to encounter in the area where he is planning to go shooting, and to be able to distinguish them from protected birds that may share the same habitat. Accurate quarry recognition is absolutely essential, and it must be perfected not only in broad daylight, but in the half-light of dawn and dusk, which is when most wildfowling takes place. Experienced wildfowlers are able instantly to recognise their quarry from its silhouette, its call and

> Experienced wildfowlers are able instantly to recognise their quarry from its silhouette, its call and even the sound of its wingbeats.

even the sound of its wingbeats. To do this takes time, and although it is possible to learn a great deal from a good book on bird identification, there is no substitute for patient hours of watching wildfowl in the company of an expert.

There can be no excuse for shooting at a protected species, and if there is any doubt in your mind whatsoever as to a bird's identity, then hold your fire.

There are, however, certain points of guidance that will help you to distinguish between the various species. Ducks can be divided into two categories, namely the diving ducks and the surface feeding, or 'dabbling' ducks. Divers feed on invertebrate creatures that they find at the bottom of deep water, either big tidal estuaries, reservoirs or deep ponds. They are characterised by a slightly dumpy appearance, and their legs and paddles are set far back along their bodies to assist them when swimming under water. When in flight the diving ducks have a distinctively rapid wingbeat. The diving ducks that may be shot are tufted duck, pochard and goldeneye. Dabbling ducks feed on or from the surface of the water, or graze upon vegetation close to the water's edge. They have an elegant, streamlined outline, and are masters of the air. Most of the duck that are commonly shot by wildfowlers are dabblers, and because they tend to be vegetarian in habit, they make the best birds for the table. The mallard is the best known of the quarry species in this group, and is universally recognisable. Other species are the wigeon, pintail, gadwall, shoveller and the teal, unmistakable because of its small size. The quarry geese comprise the pink-footed and white-fronted goose, both of which are entirely wild and migratory; the Canada goose, a feral species that has spread extensively from birds introduced to Britain in previous centuries to grace the ornamental lakes of great estates; and the greylag goose, Britain's only native breeding goose species. Canadas are easily distinguished by their great size, their long black necks and white cheek bars. The other species, or 'grey geese' are more easily distinguished in flight by their calls. To these species may be added the feral Egyptian goose, which has spread rapidly in recent years and which may be shot under certain circumstances to prevent damage or disease.

All wildfowl of whatever sort must be positively identified before they are shot at, and must never be confused with protected birds.

MALLARD

The ubiquitous mallard is found throughout the northern hemisphere, and is the ancestor of all our farmyard breeds. With its bottle green head, bright yellow bill, white neck band and blue-and-white speculum, the mallard drake is immediately familiar. He is accompanied by his more sober-hued mate, whose plumage is brown, but who still carries the blue-and-white speculum on her wings.

Mallard are found wherever there is water, on rivers, lakes, marshes and estuaries, and, of course, in urban parks, where they become very tame. They breed throughout Britain, producing ten to twelve eggs in a down-lined nest hidden close to the water's edge at any time from midwinter

onwards, though many early broods fail to survive to maturity. In winter, the 'home bred' population is augmented by very large numbers of migratory mallard from Scandinavia, Iceland and the Baltic.

Preferring to feed in shallow water, mallard eat a wide variety of vegetable food, from grain to the exposed stems of water plants. They will quickly take advantage of frosted potatoes or spoiled grain left in the fields after harvest. Like all ducks, they are masters of the air, but can easily be called by imitation of their quacking note, or attracted by the use of decoys.

TEAL

The little teal is the smallest of the commonly encountered ducks. Their diminutive size makes them instantly recognisable, and they can only be confused in the very early part of the shooting season with the protected garganey, a summer migrant. The drake teal has a grey back, a speckled breast and a gorgeous chestnut head with

broad green eye stripe. His mate is brown, but shares his iridescent green speculum.

A few thousand pairs of teal breed in Britain, but the vast majority of birds that we see in winter are migrants, with many coming from Scandinavia, Russia and Iceland. They may be found together in large numbers, are very agile in flight, and when startled will rocket vertically into the air at great speed. Teal are largely seed feeders, and prefer to dabble for the seeds of marsh grasses and sedges, though they will also take invertebrates, especially in summer. Their note, which they make in flight, is a soft but distinctive 'teep'.

WIGEON

Often considered the wildfowler's quarry par excellence, the wigeon is almost entirely a winter visitor to Britain, arriving from late August through to mid November from its breeding grounds in Scandinavia, northern Russia and Iceland. The cock is particularly handsome, in his grey plumage with white underparts, pink breast and chestnut head with brilliant sulphur-yellow forehead flash, while the hen shares her partner's grey bill with black tip and metallic green and black speculum.

The wigeon is a grazing bird, which feeds on shallow flooded meadows and tidal flashes. It also occurs in large numbers where there is plenty of its favourite saltwater food, zostera or eelgrass. Wigeon are quick to exploit freshly flooded water meadows in late autumn and winter, and where the habitat is right, tens of thousands of birds can congregate on a single site.

The familiar whistling call 'wheeoo' is made by the cock birds both in flight and on the ground, while the hens contribute a low growling sound. Wigeon are very gregarious and, under the right circumstances, are easily decoyed.

PINTAIL

This elegant and strikingly beautiful bird is one of the most abundant duck species worldwide. The female shares the graceful, elegant shape of the drake, but her grey-brown colouration cannot compare with his handsome chocolate brown head and white neck stripes. Nor does she have the highly distinctive long and pointed black tail feathers from which the species derives its name.

Pintail breed in a few isolated sites in Britain, but are mainly winter migrants, arriving in the autumn from western Scandinavia, northern Russia and Iceland, to overwinter mainly on coastal sites around the major estuary systems, particularly in the west of the country. The pintail feeds largely on aquatic plant material, but also takes invertebrates such as water insects, molluscs and worms.

The species is very familiar to the wildfowler, and can easily be recognised in flight by its long outstretched neck and its long tail, coupled with its black and white colouration.

GREYLAG GOOSE

Britain's only native breeding wild goose species, the greylag is the ancestor of most of our domestic geese. It occurs throughout the western Palearctic zone, through central Siberia to Japan, although most of the migratory greylags arriving in this country in the autumn breed mainly in Iceland, with a few birds coming from western Scandinavia and the Baltic coast. Home-bred greylags tend to remain fairly local in their habits, with significant concentrations of birds staying resident in the areas where they were raised.

It is not easy visually to distinguish the greylag from the other grey geese at a distance, although identification marks to watch for are the pale grey-brown plumage

of the head and neck, which extends down over the breast, and the orange-pink bill. Its voice, however, is distinctive: a deep bell-like 'aang ung-ung', which it makes in flight.

Natural grazers and foragers, greylags are partial to a wide range of agricultural crops, from grass through root crops and potatoes to winter cereals, something that brings them into conflict with the farmer but which can also present decoying possibilities to the wildfowler.

PINK-FOOTED GOOSE

A species that never fails to stir the fowler's heart when it arrives in the autumn from its breeding grounds in Spitzbergen, Iceland and Greenland, the pink-footed goose or 'pinkfoot' is the smallest of our grey geese, and together with the greylag, one of the two that the wildfowler will be most likely to encounter.

It can be distinguished from the greylag by its size, by its browner head and neck, and by its pink and brown bill. In flight, however, its characteristic call, a bright 'ink-ink', is a ready point of identification.

Like the greylag, it feeds largely on farmland, close to traditional coastal roosting sites such as the northern firths, the Tay and Forth valleys, the Lancashire coast, the Wash, and north and east Norfolk. It readily takes gleanings off the autumn stubbles before turning to grass, winter cereals, sugar beet tops and roots. Where vegetables are grown, pinkfeet also feed on carrots and a variety of brassica crops, often in very large flocks. Inevitably, this brings them into conflict with agriculture. As with the other grey goose species, the pinkfoot is steadily increasing in numbers, and the population is currently buoyant.

CANADA GOOSE

Nobody could possibly mistake the massive Canada goose for anything else. It is our biggest quarry bird, and with its black neck, white cheek patches and grey-brown body plumage, it is immediately recognisable. In flight, Canadas make a distinctive 'a-honk' note, which carries over long distances.

This goose is not native to Britain, but was introduced from America in the 1600s as an ornamental bird. It spread from the park lakes where it was first released, and has now become well established throughout the country. In particular it has exploited as breeding sites many of the newly created lakes that have resulted from gravel extraction. The species is also commonly seen in city parks.

Canadas feed largely on grass, and are very domineering birds. This makes them unpopular with park owners, who increasingly express concern at the way they damage and soil the lawns around ornamental lakes.

Clothing and equipment

Wildfowling is a specialised branch of shooting that calls for specialised equipment and clothing. Because wildfowlers often take shots close to the maximum effective range of the conventional 12-bore shotgun, and because wildfowl are well protected by thick layers of feathers and down, it is best to select a gun that is capable of handling heavy, high-velocity loads. Although a standard 70mm chambered 12-bore is well suited to most wildfowling situations, many dedicated wildfowlers opt for a long chambered semi-auto shotgun that is capable of handling high performance steel shot cartridges. The 10-bore has a following amongst goose shooters as it is capable of packing even heavier loads, and there are still a few diehard traditionalists who are prepared to carry a mighty 8-bore gun on the marsh. A wildfowling gun

As wildfowl are well protected by thick layers of feathers and down, it is best to select a gun that is capable of handling heavy, high-velocity loads.

must be strong, robust and preferably without any frills, for it will have to operate in wet or muddy conditions. Below the sea wall the salty atmosphere is particularly corrosive, and the foreshore is no place to take a fine, expensive shotgun.

Wildfowlers use larger shot sizes than game or rough shooters since these, when coupled with the heavier loads of the standard wildfowling cartridges, maintain more pellet energy – and thus duck-stopping power – at longer ranges. Furthermore, when steel shot is being used, a larger shot size must in any case be employed to compensate for steel's relatively low density. Clothing for wildfowling must be warm and waterproof. If you are planning to wait for ducks beside a pond or river after a day's rough shooting, then an extra fleece or sweater under your shooting jacket will probably suffice, but for serious wildfowling on the marsh or estuary you will need rather more than this. Firstly, waders or thigh boots are essential. It is a good idea to get a pair that is a size too big for you, and then to wear extra thick seaboot stockings, plus insulated liners or a pair of ankle length 'wellie socks' for extra warmth. Do make sure, however, that the extra socks

Be prepared for mud when shooting on the foreshore.

completely fill that spare space in the feet of your waders so that your boots fit tightly. If you are wearing thigh boots, then a pair of waterproof over-trousers will keep your bottom dry should you wish to sit down. A good plan is to cut the legs off, so creating a pair of waterproof 'shorts' which may be worn over your waders. Where not too much walking is to be done or if there is deep water to negotiate, then a good alternative is a pair of neoprene chest waders.

The wildfowler prays for wind and hard weather.

Keeping warm can be a problem when out wildfowling, as you may need to remain stationary for long periods. So when the weather is severe, be sure to start off with clothing that retains your body's heat. The secret is to wear several thin layers under your waterproof coat. These will trap layers of air and provide excellent insulation without creating so much bulk that you are unable to mount and swing your gun. Remember also that while long underwear may not be the height of fashion in everyday wear, it is never out of place on the marsh. Indeed, most serious wildfowlers wouldn't be without their long johns and long-sleeved vests in midwinter. A tough windproof and waterproof shooting coat worn over a fleece is ideal for wildfowling, and it is sensible to add a towelling choker in wet weather to keep the rain from trickling down your neck. As is the case with rough shooting, a hat is essential to retain your body heat and ensure that your face can be hidden from wary wildfowl. Wildfowling jackets are often supplied with a hood. While hoods will help to keep out the rain and snow, they may also restrict your visibility and a hood will almost certainly limit your ability to hear incoming birds. In cold conditions, a pair of thermally insulated shooting gloves or mittens will be very welcome.

If you try to walk across soft, estuarine mud in loose-fitting boots, they will be sucked off in an instant, as many a novice wildfowler has learned to his cost.

There may be occasions when you will have to walk a long distance from where you park your car to the place where you will be shooting. If this is the case, then it is a good idea to keep a layer of warm clothing, such as a fleece, in your bag during your outward journey. A half hour walk across rough country will most likely make you work up quite a sweat, even on a freezing cold morning, and if you then sit still for a couple of hours in a pool of perspiration, you really will get cold. Far better to keep comfortable while walking into position, then add another layer before you settle down and wait for the birds to start moving.

A capacious game bag is very useful when wildfowling. First, it will be needed to carry all those extra little bits of kit that are necessary on the marsh, and second, it will be useful to sit on. Finally, it will come in handy if you should be so lucky as to shoot a duck or a goose. Choose one with two compartments; in this way you can keep wet, muddy things like camouflage nets and dead ducks separate from your sandwiches and Thermos flask.

Waiting for geese on the winter marshes.

A pair of binoculars is very useful when out wildfowling, enabling you to identify birds at long range, and so adding a great deal of extra interest to your visit to the marsh. There's no need for a big expensive pair of binoculars – a pocket-sized pair of roof-prism glasses will do fine. A pen knife and a three-part set of cleaning rods will help you with running repairs or removing mud from your gun barrels, while a long, stout wading stick will allow you to test the depth of the water as you cross flooded creeks or ditches.

Safety equipment is vital. Carry your mobile phone and make sure it is fully charged before setting out. Hand-held GPS devices can guide you safely onto the marsh and get you off again in poor visibility, but failing one of these, carry a compass and know how to use it. It is no joke to be lost on a strange marsh with a rising tide and a dense blanket of fog all about you. In these circumstances, your GPS or compass can be a real life-saver. A whistle may be used to call for help if you drop your mobile phone in the water or the battery fails, and a hand-held yachtsman's flare is worth keeping in your bag to attract attention in a real emergency or if you find there is no mobile phone signal.

Hand-held GPS devices can guide you safely onto the marsh and get you off again in poor visibility, but failing one of these, carry a compass and know how to use it.

Some form of illumination is important. Either use your mobile phone or carry a small torch in your bag. It can be invaluable when you are looking for a lost bird or trying to find your way home in the dark, and in an emergency it will help a potential rescuer to locate you. A head torch enables you to see where you are going or what you are doing while leaving your hands free. However, do not use your torch any more than is absolutely necessary, especially before morning flight, as a flashing light on the marsh may disturb wildfowl.

Flighting

Most wildfowlers try to intercept ducks and geese as they travel between their feeding and their resting or roosting grounds. Under normal circumstances, ducks feed at dawn and dusk, and roost during the day on open water or in the security of ponds or reed beds. Geese, on the other hand, feed during the daylight hours and roost at night, often on sandbanks exposed by the tide. Thus, there is a natural traffic of wildfowl in the morning and evening, and these two spells of activity are known as 'morning flight' and 'evening flight'. The process of shooting wildfowl at these times, or at other periods of natural movement, is known as 'flighting'.

To flight wildfowl successfully on the open marsh requires detailed knowledge of the neighbouring feeding and roosting grounds so that you can position yourself underneath the anticipated flight line between the two. Perhaps there is a pond or lagoon where birds regularly come to feed, or from which they regularly depart at first light. Perhaps there is a river or main creek along which they prefer to fly. If so, then use these features to guide you to a suitable flighting position. Take account of the wind direction, which may well make the birds deviate from their normal route. Wind strength is also very important to the wildfowl shooter, as ducks and geese will always fly lower in a strong wind. Indeed, a howling gale is something that the coastal goose shooter prays for, since it gives him his best chance to get within range of the mighty skeins as they battle over the foreshore where he is lying in wait.

Ducks and geese will always fly lower in a strong wind.

Weather conditions are important in another respect. Hard frost is always looked forward to by wildfowlers because it concentrates wildfowl on the coast. Salt water freezes at a lower temperature than fresh water, so when the inland ponds, lakes and rivers freeze over, birds will move to the coast and congregate on tidal estuaries, giving the wildfowler a chance to get amongst bigger numbers of ducks and geese.

Having found a suitable position on the marsh or river bank, make sure that you are well hidden, either in a creek or ditch, in a clump of reeds or in a hide. Wildfowl are sharp-eyed, and will quickly spot anything amiss on the marsh. If you do not conceal yourself sufficiently well, they will give you a wide berth.

Once in position, try to face the direction from which the birds are expected, but keep checking all quarters constantly. Remember that there is nothing guaranteed about wildfowling, and ducks may come from any direction, at all ranges, speeds and altitudes. You must have

Left: Pinkfeet over! A sight to thrill any wildfowler.

Below: Mallard lifting off a coastal flight pond.

your wits about you at every moment during flight time. If you do spot a party of approaching wildfowl that you have positively identified as quarry birds, then keep out of sight and remain perfectly still until the very last moment. Any unnecessary movement or a glimpse of your face as you look up is guaranteed to make them turn away.

Arrive in plenty of time to get into position before flight begins. Remember that if you are shooting the morning flight, this will mean finding your place well before it starts getting light. Equally, do not leave the marsh until the flight is over and the birds have stopped moving or it is genuinely too dark to shoot. Unnecessary wandering across the marsh during flight time causes disturbance and is annoying and discourteous to other wildfowlers. However, if there is nobody else on the marsh then you may, of course, wish to change position to take advantage of a better flight line, and no conscientious wildfowler

Wigeon are a principal quarry of the wildfowler.

should object to you leaving your position in order to retrieve a wounded bird while the flight is in progress.

Apart from dawn and dusk, the natural cycles of tide and moon create other periods of wildfowl traffic. A daytime tide will flood the foreshore where birds may be roosting and, if the wind is sufficiently strong to make the water choppy and uncomfortable, it will force them to seek a more sheltered roosting site. By exploiting this natural movement you may be able to enjoy a 'tide flight'. As with all coastal wildfowling, it will be necessary for you to check in advance, either online or by means of a published tide table, the predicted time and height of the tide. Remember that both of these factors may be altered quite dramatically by strong winds. The main period of activity during a tide flight is when the principal roosts are flooding, often two or three hours before high water, so make sure you get into position early. Neither must you forget to leave the marsh in good time. A rapidly flooding tide may easily cut off your line of retreat.

Wildfowl will also flight at night under the influence of the full moon. Wigeon, in particular, feed by moonlight, and when the sky is veiled by a thin film of high or medium level cloud it is possible to shoot them at night. Adequate cloud cover is essential, for when duck are flying against the backdrop of a clear night sky, even under the brightest of moons, they will be completely invisible even if only a short distance away from you. Shooting by the light of a rising full moon under a brightly lit covering of dappled cloud that reaches from horizon to horizon is a particularly magical sport, made all the more precious by the handful of occasions each shooting season when moon and weather conditions combine to allow it. However, moon flighting demands excellent marsh skills and complete mastery of wildfowl identification, and it is not an activity recommended to the unaccompanied beginner.

Flight ponds

It may be that you have access to a pond or lake where wildfowl come to feed in the evening. 'Flight pond' shooting is very popular, not just with dedicated wildfowlers, but with rough shooters and game shooters

Above left: Regular feeding will bring ducks into your pond.

Above right: A September flight pond can provide great sport.

who can use a flight pond to add an extra dimension to their day's sport. Many flight ponds are deliberately 'fed' with grain, potatoes or pulses in order to attract ducks to them, and then shot throughout the season. It is recommended that such shooting should not be carried out more than once a fortnight, otherwise the ducks will start to associate the pond with danger and will desert it altogether.

If there is more than one hide around the same pond, take extreme care not to take low shots at ducks that are about to settle on the water if there is another hide anywhere near your line of fire. Shot will easily ricochet off the water.

Sometimes, ponds that are shot regularly have permanent hides built around their perimeters. These provide safe and comfortable shooting positions and ensure that the Guns are well hidden from ducks approaching the pond. If you are invited to an organised flight pond shoot, make sure that your host tells you where any other neighbouring Guns are situated. If there is more than one hide around the same pond, then take extreme care not to take low shots at ducks that are about to settle on the water if there is another hide anywhere near your line of fire. Remember that shot will easily ricochet off the water.

Flight pond shooting can be very fast and exciting sport, and it is not unknown for the very best game shots to be completely thrown by teal that zip over the tops of their hides at head height or mallard that swing over the willows and sideslip quickly down to the water in front of them. As with all wildfowl shooting in low light conditions, you must keep your wits about you, spot your birds early and if they are dropping fast, as is often the case with flight pond shooting, get your barrels well underneath them.

As the light fades, it may well be that you are only able to pick out your birds against one particular patch of sky that is lighter than the rest, such as the afterglow above the western horizon. If so, then focus all your attention on this point. Do not attempt to search about you for birds which, even if close by, are nevertheless invisible in the darkness. Concentrate instead on the one 'window' available to you, and shoot the moment the bird enters it.

While the wildfowler generally picks his birds as he shoots them, picking-up on an organised flight pond shoot is generally left until flight is over. Make a mental note, therefore, of the locations of any birds you have shot, so that nothing is left behind. And if by chance you should drop a bird onto the water which, though unable to fly, is nevertheless a lively swimmer, it is quite in order for you to despatch it by firing a second barrel at it on the water – provided, of course, that it is safe for you to do so. This can make all the difference between putting a bird in the bag and leaving a wounded one behind to suffer.

Calls and decoys

Instead of merely putting your faith in the wind and weather and hoping that the birds will fly over you, it is possible to use fieldcraft skills to bring ducks or geese close to where you are hidden. The way that wildfowlers do this is by using calls and decoys. A call imitates the sound of a duck or goose, and can be used to attract the attention of passing birds, bringing them within shooting range. Some skilled wildfowlers are able to reproduce the note of a duck or goose by using their voices entirely unaided. However, most people use an artificial call, normally made of wood, plastic or metal. Calling can be very effective, but before you try it, spend some time listening to the natural vocabulary of ducks and geese as they feed and rest, then practise imitating the notes you hear. Use calls sparingly. Don't overdo it and never call unless there are birds in the vicinity; nobody, however proficient at calling, is able to conjure birds out of thin air. Calls are often used in conjunction with decoys: artificial ducks or geese, usually made from moulded plastic and painted to look like the real thing. Wildfowl are naturally gregarious and decoys exploit their natural desire to flock together with others of their kind. When placed in a natural looking pattern on a suitable feeding ground, they can prove very effective at bringing birds down in front of the Guns. Even three or four duck decoys can make all the difference in encouraging passing birds to come in to a pond at

> The real skill in calling is to be able to judge the exact moment when a single note will bring a duck or a goose wheeling round and looking for its friends down below.

Setting out decoys on a flooded wash.

evening flight, while some wildfowlers use dozens of decoys at a time to bring wigeon in to more extensive areas of temporary flood water.

Decoys are often used by inland goose shooters, who position artificial full-bodied birds, shell decoys or even simple silhouette 'cut-outs' on a field where the geese are known to feed regularly. By skilful decoying at dawn, when the geese are coming off the roosts to feed, it is possible to bring large numbers of grey geese right down in front of the Guns to create one of the most exciting of all wildfowling opportunities.

When using decoys on water, remember that they will have to be 'rigged' with lines and anchor weights to prevent them from drifting away. Wildfowlers who regularly shoot shallow freshwater flashes often rig their decoys individually, as this offers more flexibility when building up a decoy pattern. When shooting on tidal or running water, it is generally more convenient to have several decoys rigged to a single line and anchor weight. By running the line back to the high water mark and pegging it securely, you can ensure that you can retrieve your decoys at the end of the flight, no matter how much the tide has risen.

A few well-positioned decoys can be deadly at bringing in single birds or pairs, but a larger rig of decoys is necessary when bigger packs of birds are on the move, and there is no doubt that the larger the number of decoys in your rig, the more pulling power it has. Those wildfowlers who shoot in locations where there may be large concentrations of live birds on the water only a short distance away know full well that it is pointless them taking to the marsh with only two or three decoys in their bag. Instead, they try to use all the decoys they can carry. Two dozen full-bodied duck decoys will fit quite comfortably into a decoy bag, so a couple of fowlers shooting together are quite able to make a useful spread of decoys. Some fowlers who shoot where transporting decoys is not a problem regularly shoot with rigs of up to a hundred birds, and very effective they are too.

Before the days of moulded plastic, decoys were carved out of wood and painted by hand. Old wooden decoys can sometimes still be found, and those that are in good condition can command high prices from collectors, especially in the United States where there is a long tradition of decoy carving. Wooden decoys make very attractive ornaments and decoy carving, originally practised purely for the purpose of putting more ducks in the hunter's bag, has spawned an entirely new branch of art.

The wildfowler's dog

Gundogs are central to the sport of wildfowling. While the game shooter can do perfectly well without a dog of his own, and even the rough shooter might be able to get by much of the time without one, the wildfowler is at a big disadvantage if he does not have a dog. When shooting on marshes, rivers, lakes or estuaries, there is going to come a time when a bird will drop in the water, and without a dog it is likely to be lost. Perhaps some hardy souls may be prepared to strip off and swim for a bird, but how much easier and more comfortable it is to leave the retrieving to a good water dog. At evening flight when there are wounded birds to be collected from reeds or thick waterside cover, a gundog is the only humane means of ensuring that they are quickly brought to hand and despatched, and it should be a point of honour with every wildfowler that he should at all times have a dog of his own or at least that he should have access to a dog belonging to a companion who is shooting with him.

A good dog is an essential companion.

To shoot a duck or a goose and then leave it unretrieved because you have no dog with you is not merely contrary to the ethics of the sport of wildfowling, it is a sheer waste of a precious wildlife resource.

Boats

Most wildfowling marshes are accessible on foot, but not all. For some, access is only achievable by boat. Using a boat can make the work of transporting shooting gear, hides and decoy bags much easier, or enable you to shoot on outlying marshes or islands around high water, so adding another dimension to your fowling expeditions.

In some situations, a boat can provide a shooting platform, enabling a fowler to shoot in deep floodwater or across tidal foreshore. Many fowlers who use boats for this purpose will camouflage their boat to make it less conspicuous. A can of green or brown paint is useful, along with sections of camo net that can be fixed in position so that the boat becomes, in effect, a floating hide. Purpose-built kayaks have been used by sea anglers for a number of years, and are now proving themselves popular with wildfowlers. They are light, quick to launch and may be carried easily on a car roof. They can operate in very shallow water and on big, flooded marshes a kayak can open up lots of new shooting opportunities.

There are a few points to note about using a boat for wildfowling. Firstly, the law prohibits the use of a mechanically propelled vehicle, including a boat, in immediate pursuit of wildfowl. So, although you may, for example, use an outboard motor if you are using a boat simply to get to a location from which you intend to shoot, no motor is permitted on a boat that is used as a shooting platform. Furthermore, if you plan to shoot from a boat after having used an outboard motor to get into position, then it is best to unship the motor or lift it out of the water before you start to shoot, so that there can be no suggestion that you are shooting while under power. 'Immediate pursuit' may also apply to the retrieval of dead or wounded birds, so if necessary ensure that you have a pair of oars, a paddle, pole or some other manual means of propulsion.

> Dogs are very vulnerable in the water, and a number of accidents have occurred when a swimming dog is 'run over' by a fowler's boat under power from an outboard motor.

Boats introduce an additional range of safety issues. It should go without saying that in high winds, heavy seas or strong currents there may be significant dangers. Nor is it any fun at all to be locked in pack ice on a freezing estuary on an ebb tide with an offshore wind. Take great care with boats; if appropriate use an inflatable lifejacket and if you are fowling on tidal waters, then keep a yachtsman's flare in your shooting bag. Make sure your dog is safe, warm and comfortable too.

Boats make good shooting platforms and are invaluable for carrying fowling gear and decoys out to your shooting position – or ducks on the homeward journey.

A further branch of waterborne wildfowling deserves mention, if only because of the central place it holds in the history of the sport. Punt gunning involves the use of a one- or two-man gunning punt, looking not unlike a canoe, upon which is mounted a large-calibre shotgun. The object is to stalk undetected into large groups of wildfowl, usually while they are resting on exposed tidal mudbanks, and take a flock or group shot at close range. Punt gunning is an extremely specialised activity that has remained essentially unchanged over more than a century and takes a great deal of experience to master. It is also a very arduous sport, taking place in the remotest parts of our estuaries, usually in the very depths of winter. It requires both a high degree of fitness, fieldcraft, navigation skills and local knowledge of the movements of wildfowl. Punt gunning has been the core activity of some of wildfowling's greatest figures, and those who take part in it often regard it as the cream of all wildfowling.

Wildfowling opportunity

Wildfowl shooting inland has always been controlled, like every other form of sporting shooting, by owners and occupiers of land. On the

Waiting for tide flight on the snow-bound estuary.

CHAPTER 8

Pigeon shooting

PIGEON SHOOTING

THE CONTROL of farm pests has always been an important aspect of shooting, and if the rough shooter obtains his sport by courtesy of a local farmer, then the killing of rabbits or winged vermin is one way in which he can help prevent damage to valuable crops. The control of one farm pest, however, has grown into a specialised form of shooting in its own right. Pigeon shooting may be looked upon by the arable farmer as a means of defending his fields against the depredations of the grey flocks, but thousands of shooters recognise it as a uniquely challenging sport in which the use of fieldcraft and first-rate shooting skills must be combined in order for success to be achieved.

The need for pest control

Pigeons are recognised as Britain's number one bird pest on the farm, indeed, researchers believe that in some cases the pigeon wreaks more devastation even than insect pests. On the important and valuable break crop of oilseed rape, it is not unknown for farmers to experience

Pigeon damage to young cabbages. Woodpigeons are Britain's number one farm bird pest.

losses of up to forty per cent of their final expected yields as a result of attacks by pigeons. Other brassica crops such as cabbages and Brussels sprouts are equally susceptible to pigeon damage, and even if their yield is not greatly depressed, pecking and the depositing of droppings by feeding pigeons will almost certainly mean that a vegetable crop is unsaleable.

The scale of the damage to individual crops is greatly influenced by the timing of a pigeon raid. Major concentrations of birds grazing on rape between November and early January appear to make little difference to the tonnage of rapeseed that finds its way into the combine harvester. Grazing from late January to March, though, is much more serious, and it is at this stage of late winter and early spring that most of the long-term damage is done. Shooting of even very large numbers of pigeons probably has little overall effect on the bird's population, but at the level of the individual farm, shooting can be very effective in keeping pigeons from feeding on a particular field, and it is for this reason that many farmers welcome responsible pigeon shooters, especially those who are prepared to turn out at a moment's notice when crops are under siege.

Pigeons are recognised as Britain's number one bird pest on the farm. It is not unknown for farmers to experience losses of up to forty per cent of their final expected yields as a result of attacks by pigeons.

Brassica crops, peas, beans and cereals are all susceptible to attack by the woodpigeon.

Quarry species

The central character on the pigeon shooting scene is the woodpigeon, which is recognisable by the distinctive white patches on each side of its neck and its white wing bars. A woodpigeon's flight is deceptive. One moment it may appear to be flapping lazily towards you, but the instant it spots danger it will jink and accelerate away with a display of aerobatic expertise that will defy even the most experienced of shots. Pigeon shooters may also encounter the feral pigeon. This legal quarry bird is descended from generations of domesticated pigeons that have been released or that have escaped from captivity. It is smaller than the woodpigeon and has a wide variety of markings. Feral pigeons may cause considerable crop damage, but the shooter should only tackle them when they are indeed raiding the farmer's crops, as feral pigeons are indistinguishable from the domestic birds from which they originated, and it is all too easy accidentally to shoot a valuable racing or domestic pigeon that has the misfortune of choosing to fly over your hide. For this reason, most pigeon shooters wisely concentrate their attention solely on the woodpigeon.

The only other species that is related to the woodpigeon and that may legally be shot is the collared dove, a bird of the farmyard and grain store that feeds on spilled grain. It is a delicately built bird with a pale cinnamon colouring and a distinctive dark collar around its neck. The stock dove is smaller than the woodpigeon, blue-grey in colour and with a glossy green neck, but no white neck patches. It is protected and may not be shot.

Tactics and timing

Pigeon shooting is geared closely to the farming calendar. In winter, as we have seen, it is the brassica crops such as oilseed rape that attract pigeons in large numbers. When there is snow on the ground and the pigeons are really hungry, they may feed on any brassica crop that is exposed above the snow in an almost suicidal manner. Brassica leaves, however, have a relatively poor food value, and it will take a pigeon a considerable while to eat and digest the amount of leaf material necessary to provide it with the energy it needs to survive. At other times of the year this energy is much more readily obtained from other sources.

Spring

In spring, fresh sowings of cereals, peas and beans are irresistible to pigeons, and they will eat not merely those seeds that are left lying on the surface of the field by the seed drill, but will dig along the rows and remove large numbers of seeds. Newly germinated peas are also raided mercilessly by pigeons, as are the fresh young shoots of clover.

Summer

In summer, pigeons will feast off fields of ripening cereals, especially barley or wheat that has been 'laid' or knocked over before harvest by strong winds or heavy rain, and the moment the corn is cut, pigeons will descend onto the stubbles to mop up the spilled grain. After the cereals have been harvested, it is time for the field beans to be combined, producing another feeding bonanza for pigeons.

Autumn

Then, when the autumn cultivations start, they can be seen on the newly drilled crops of autumn cereals.

Each of these situations provides an opportunity for the pigeon shooter, for pigeons are truly a year-round quarry. It therefore pays dividends to know and understand the patterns of cropping in the area where you intend to shoot, and to observe closely what the birds are feeding on at any one time. If you attempt to shoot over one crop while the pigeons prefer to feed on something entirely different, then you will have a very frustrating time, and you will be unlikely to shoot many pigeons.

Clothing and equipment

A rough shooter's standard clothing and equipment will be in most cases entirely suitable for pigeon shooting. A conventional 12-bore double-barrelled gun is ideal, although many shooters who operate

Camouflaged clothing and a face mask will help to prevent you from being spotted by sharp-eyed pigeons.

out of the confined space of a pigeon hide prefer the convenience of a semi-auto, since it does not have to be broken for reloading. Bear in mind the fact that when pigeon decoying for extended periods, you may well be firing quite large numbers of cartridges, so ensure that the gun is a comfortable fit, and that recoil is not excessive with the cartridge that you are proposing to use. A pigeon shooter's clothing will need to be appropriate to the prevailing weather conditions. In midwinter, conventional winter rough shooting kit will be required, with perhaps an extra fleece or sweater if you are expecting to be seated motionless in a hide for long periods. Likewise, in high summer, you may find that you are shooting in shirt sleeves. If so, ensure that your shirt is of an appropriately sober colouring, and if necessary wear a skeet vest to assist with gun mounting and to make shooting more comfortable against the shoulder.

A hat is, of course, essential, and some shooters go so far as to wear a face mask or veil. Certainly, these are extremely effective, but they can also be very uncomfortable and awkward to shoot in unless you are well used to them.

Decoying

Although most shooters at some time in the season will shoot the odd pigeon whilst walking along a hedgerow, standing at a pheasant drive or even crouching in a creek on a salt marsh, the vast majority of pigeons are shot over decoys. Like wildfowl, pigeons are gregarious by nature, and like to feed in the company of their fellows. Decoying exploits this habit by creating the illusion of a contented flock of birds feeding happily on their favourite food, the objective being to extend an open invitation to any passing pigeon to join in the feast. Pigeons, however, are not stupid, and the decoy picture has to be totally realistic if it is to do the job intended of it.

As we have seen, it is no use spreading your decoys over a crop on which the pigeons simply do not wish to feed. Neither is there any point

Left: Shell decoy.

Middle: Full-bodied plastic decoy.

Right: Natural bird.

in positioning decoys in a place where there is no passing pigeon traffic to spot them: it is essential before committing yourself to decoying in one particular spot to establish the route of the flight lines being used by pigeons travelling back and forth between their feeding grounds and the resting sites, such as tall hedgerow trees and small copses, where the birds sit quietly to digest their food.

Timing is as important as geography. There is no point in trying to tempt pigeons down from the sky when there are none there in the first place. Pigeon feed at certain times of day, and only when they are actually interested in feeding will you draw them down to the decoys. During the short, dark days of winter this is not so much of an issue, since the birds will most likely need to spend the greater part of the daylight hours gathering whatever food is available, especially if that food is of relatively low nutritional value. At other times of the year, however, feeding periods are concentrated at different times of the day. Pigeon normally like to feed first thing in the morning, just after dawn, following which there is a spell of inactivity before the main feeding session starts, often at around midday. The birds then normally feed throughout the afternoon, putting in a particularly active burst of gorging before they go up to roost at dusk. Of course, these times may vary according to local conditions, the weather and the quality of the feeding available, but the most consistent time for decoying is probably from midday through to the late afternoon.

Pigeon feed at certain times of day, and only when they are actually interested in feeding will you draw them down to the decoys.

When setting out decoys for pigeons, your aim will be to reproduce as closely as possible the picture of a carefree flock of feeding birds. Most pigeons feed facing into the wind, and although you should not position your decoys in too regimented a manner, the majority should indeed be head-to-wind. They should also be well spaced out, leaving one or more inviting 'holes' into which guests can drop. Your aim will be to invite passing birds to come in to a 'killing zone' around twenty-five metres from your hide.

There is no doubt that the best decoys are dead birds, and many serious pigeon shooters keep a few preserved pigeons to act as the main body of their decoy pattern, or use birds that they have shot a day or so previously. Most shooters, however, use commercially available artificial decoys, of which there are several excellent styles, ranging from the full-bodied plastic type to the 'shell' decoy, which, though it looks less realistic, has the advantage of being lighter and taking up less space in your decoy bag. In many situations artificial decoys will do an excellent job, but in strong sunlight their shiny upper surfaces do tend to reflect more light than a genuine bird, thus sending a warning signal to any approaching pigeon that something is not quite right.

Decoys should be carefully set out to look like feeding pigeons with the majority facing the wind.

Some pigeon shooters overcome this by cutting the wings off a dead pigeon and then gluing them to an artificial bird. Though the idea may sound a little strange, this trick can work very well. Plastic decoys are also available with a flock finish to prevent reflection. As your tally mounts during the course of a shoot, you should replace your artificial decoys with genuine dead birds.

Whatever decoys you are using, however, it is important to ensure that they are easily visible from the air. This is achieved by mounting them on short sticks, so that they are not hidden by the crop on which they are supposed to be feeding. Some proprietary decoys when thus mounted will rock back and forth in a gentle breeze, simulating a realistic pecking action. Likewise, each dead bird should be carefully set out to look like a feeding pigeon, its head supported either by a short forked twig or by a longer, pointed stick pushed into the base of its lower mandible.

The white wing markings that a pigeon displays as it settles act as a powerful signal to any birds that might be watching that there is food to be had, and pigeon shooters seek to exploit this fact by using a 'cradle'. This is a device that consists of a long springy stem, topped

A cradle holds this natural bird well above a crop of young peas where it is visible to passing pigeon traffic.

> A decoy pattern is basically a static creation, and the addition of movement can often be the final touch which draws in the birds.

with an arrangement of wire into which a dead pigeon may be fixed with its wings spread. When correctly positioned in the cradle, the dead pigeon looks exactly as though it is just about to touch down amongst the rest of the decoy pattern. In addition, the lightest of breezes will make it rock realistically.

Despite decoys that rock in the wind, a decoy pattern is basically a static creation, and the addition of movement can often be the final touch which draws in the birds. The objective, just as with the use of a static cradle, is to simulate a pigeon that is just settling to feed amongst its contented fellows, and this can be achieved by placing a dead bird in a 'flapper' cradle, which can be operated either manually by a string running back to the hide or by a small electric motor which, when the cradle is operated, opens the pigeon's wings to expose the white wing bars in a flash of movement to attract any passing birds. Also very popular is the 'pigeon magnet,' which consists of a couple of cradles that take dead birds with their wings spread open. These are connected to a central spindle driven by an electric motor. The effect is that of two pigeons circling close to the

A pigeon magnet driven by a small electric motor can prove a deadly addition to the pigeon shooter's armoury.

Try to let the birds come into the killing zone over your decoys before shooting.

ground prior to settling, and it can be very effective in drawing passing birds from a long distance.

Technology can be very effective, but it is best to use it with a light touch. And if you don't want to go to the expense of buying an electric flapper or pigeon magnet, then you can always try the old trick of lobbing a dead pigeon out of the hide and into your decoys just as a likely looking bird is passing by. However, if you are to make this work, your timing has got to be perfect.

A further refinement to the decoy pattern is the addition of 'lofters', pigeon decoys mounted in high trees close to your decoy spread. These simulate the birds that have enjoyed a tasty snack and are presently digesting their food before dropping down once more to rejoin their comrades. Lofters are easily visible to passing pigeons, and act as a signal to them to take a closer look. There are two ways of lofting decoys. The first is by throwing a weight attached to a length of strong fishing line over a convenient branch, then attaching a full-bodied decoy to the other end of the line and pulling it up into position before tying it off. The second is by using sectioned lightweight lofting poles. Lofters are effective, but do not use them anywhere near overhead power lines.

Hide construction

Attracting passing pigeons is only one side of the decoying story. The other is ensuring that you are perfectly concealed until it is too late for the visiting pigeon to discover that it has just made a very bad mistake. Hide construction is therefore an integral part of the fieldcraft associated with pigeon shooting. The best possible hide is a natural one composed of materials that are to be found in the field where you are decoying, or one that simulates something that the pigeons will not associate with danger. Simplest is the hedgerow hide, which can be created in a few minutes with a billhook or a pair of loppers or secateurs, provided that your farmer host is happy with this. Alternatively, he may be prepared to deposit a number of straw bales with which you can construct the warmest and most luxurious of all pigeon hides, a bale hide, which the birds will take for nothing more than a harmless straw stack. A variant of this at harvest time is to shoot from a parked farm trailer loaded with straw bales, a fortress of a hide that gives you the added advantage of height.

If you are unable to use natural materials, then you will have to bring your own, and the most commonly used are a set of portable hide poles and a camouflage net. These can be very effective under most circumstances, although if it is very windy, then the camouflage netting can flap alarmingly. Make sure also that it is of a colour that matches the surrounding herbage. A dark olive green camo net will stick out a mile against the pale straw colours of dead winter grasses.

Whatever you make your hide of, though, ensure that it has a high back so that when you rise to shoot, your head is not silhouetted against its rim. If you do not take this simple precaution, then the jack-in-the-box effect as you bob up to take a shot will instantly startle the approaching bird, so presenting you with a far more difficult shot than might otherwise have been the case. Surprisingly, pigeons will often take little notice of the sound of your shooting, provided that you remain well hidden. Most experienced pigeon shooters will confirm that one bird may sometimes be killed while a second is coming in to the decoys and that, provided the shooter

A bale hide is the warmest and most luxurious of all pigeon hides and one which the birds will take for nothing more than a harmless straw stack.

Left: The best hide is a natural one, built from local materials.

Below: A pigeon's eye view. This shooter is well concealed.

remains concealed, the following bird will take no notice of the noise and can hopefully be bagged too. It seems that, with today's widespread use of gas bangers for bird scaring, pigeons do not necessarily connect loud bangs with danger, and can mistake a bird falling to your shot for one that is simply eager to land and feed.

Retrieving pigeons

You should regularly pick up your dead birds during a shoot. While dead pigeons, when properly pegged out, make the most effective decoys, when crumpled on the ground amidst a heap of white feathers, they are likely to send the wrong signals to any approaching birds. When the coast is clear, retrieve them, and if there is a lull in the action,

Pick up your birds regularly. Stray white feathers from a dead pigeon may warn incoming birds that something is amiss.

set them out amongst your decoys and perhaps bring in one or more of your artificial decoys in exchange. It goes without saying that if you have a wounded bird down on the ground in front of you, you must go out and despatch it immediately, whatever other pigeon traffic might be following it.

While on the subject of retrieving pigeons, a pigeon hide is one place in the shooting field in which it is not always necessary to have a gundog. Indeed, many experienced pigeon shooters prefer not to have their hide encumbered by a dog, especially when they are decoying over bare, freshly drilled fields where there is no cover in which a fallen bird may be lost. In all other circumstances, humanity dictates that a dog should be available in order quickly to find any wounded bird that is not easily visible. Even so, some farmers might be unhappy about pigeon shooters' dogs hunting for missing birds amongst fields of lodged cereals before harvest. If your farmer host definitely says that he does not want you to bring your dog, then you must try to ensure that every bird is killed cleanly, and avoid taking anything but the easiest of shots. Alternatively, there is no dishonour in declining the invitation to shoot: the woodpigeon may be an agricultural pest, but it still deserves your respect, and should not be allowed to lie wounded and unrecovered.

Roost shooting

Although not nearly so effective in killing large quantities of pigeons as decoying, there is another aspect of pigeon shooting that offers superb sport. Roost shooting is carried out late in the afternoon and into the evening as the birds, having finished feeding for the day, return to roost in woodlands close to their feeding grounds. Pigeon roosting woods can easily be identified through a little local reconnaissance, and if you have a roosting wood on your shoot or can obtain permission to shoot in one from the farmer or landowner, then make sure that you try this exciting form of pigeon shooting.

Organised roost shoots are often held on Saturdays in February, shortly after the end of the game shooting season, and when there are shooters operating in most of the local roosting woods and the pigeons are thus kept on the move, shooting can continue until it is dark. Even within a favoured wood, there will be certain trees or groups of trees in which the pigeons will prefer to roost, and you should try to identify these before going shooting. A block of evergreen conifers in a mixed woodland is often sought after by pigeons, since it provides extra warmth and shelter, especially during bitter winter weather. Tall groups of trees are also favoured, as they make excellent vantage points from which the birds may spot danger. Having located a likely looking part of your roosting wood, and having got there well before dusk, try to find a spot where you can stand with your back to a tree and shoot through a gap or opening in the woodland canopy. When the roosting flight commences, try to spot your birds as they approach, and take them as they zip across your gap. It is easier said than done, especially in a strong wind.

Below left: When roost shooting try to ignore the twigs and branches around and concentrate only on the pigeon.

Below right: Roost shooting in late winter offers superb sport.

An important point to remember when you are roost shooting, is that you should try to ignore the tracery of twigs and branches around you and concentrate only on the pigeon at which you are shooting. If you swing with the bird and shoot through the twigs, the chances are that you will be successful. Do not, however, try to shoot at birds that are out of range. Too often, inexperienced pigeon shooters blast away at birds that are far above the treetops and way out of range. This only serves to scare off any birds that may be following, spoiling the sport of any other shooter waiting nearby. It is also a waste of cartridges.

> In snowy weather pigeons will be anxious to tuck well into the roosting woods and may come to roost in large numbers.

A good time to shoot roosting pigeons is in the snow. In snowy weather pigeons will be particularly anxious to tuck well into the roosting woods and may come to roost in large numbers. Like other birds, they also tend to find snow dazzling and disorientating and so may fail to spot a waiting pigeon shooter. A windy evening can also be a very good one on which to go roost shooting, as the wind tends to keep the birds constantly on the move.

At all times when roost shooting remain quiet and still, keeping yourself as well camouflaged as possible amongst the trees. A few strands of camouflage netting may help you if there is little natural cover on the woodland floor. If by any chance a pigeon should settle within range of where you are standing, then remember that one of the objectives of pigeon shooting is pest control, and so do not hesitate to shoot. However, make sure you aim for the feet, as otherwise you will see your 'sitter' fly off into the sunset.

CHAPTER 9

Gundogs

GUNDOGS

DOGS have been among man's closest hunting companions since the dawn of time. Early hunters used dogs to assist them in taking wild animals, and the first farmers used them to guard livestock. Over the centuries the dog's basic instincts to find, chase, catch and carry game have been carefully refined and channelled by generations of selective breeding. Fundamental to the dog's value as a hunting partner are both its speed and the fact that its sense of smell is infinitely more powerful than that of a human being. Dogs are therefore able to locate game at a distance by detecting its airborne smell or 'scent', and to hunt animals or birds by following the scent trail that they leave on vegetation or on the ground.

This wonderful combination of speed and scenting ability was brought to perfection with the development of hunting hounds, which were and are still bred to hunt as a pack in order to pursue a trail or

Experienced dogs will watch every bird and mark precisely the fall of game.

the line of a quarry. Other hunting dogs, the 'gaze hounds' were bred to bring down their quarry by speed alone. Their modern descendants are breeds like the greyhound and saluki. A third type of dog was required for the ancient sport of falconry, where it was necessary first to locate game and then flush it on command for the hawk or falcon to chase, and it was from the pointing dogs bred by the old-time falconers that many of our modern gundog breeds descend. The introduction of the sporting gun led to the requirement for many more dogs capable of using their sensitive noses to find and flush game and then to retrieve dead birds or animals after they had been shot by the hunter. These tasks of finding, flushing and retrieving game are still the basic roles of the gundog, and over the last two hundred years they have been refined by sportsmen and dog breeders to produce the wealth of specialist gundog breeds we have today.

Why gundogs are needed

Gundogs are central to the shooting scene. In a practical sense, a dog is essential in order to locate birds or animals lurking in thick cover, and then to flush them so that the Guns are able to shoot at them. Without a dog to hunt game out with its nose, many birds would simply crouch low in the undergrowth and would never be spotted by Guns or beaters. Hunting and flushing dogs therefore make a major contribution to the shooter's chances of putting game in the bag, and without the presence of one or more well trained dogs, anyone wishing to shoot in even relatively light cover will be at a big disadvantage.

One of the objectives of shooting is to produce food for the table, so when the bird or animal is shot, it has to be found and retrieved.

One of the objectives of shooting is to produce food for the table, so when the bird or animal is shot, it has to be found and retrieved. That may be an easy task if it is lying dead in an open field beside your peg on a driven shoot. More often, though, it will have fallen in the depths of some thicket or maybe into the middle of a tidal river, and to recover it without a dog could mean hours of patient searching or a long, cold swim. Perhaps more importantly, it will sometimes happen that a bird or animal is only wounded by your shot. Wounded game is

Throughout your shooting career, a gundog will increase the pleasure you get from your sport many times over.

The Labrador retriever is the most popular of the working gundog breeds.

surprisingly strong, especially when only lightly struck in the wing. It will often very quickly run or swim a long way from where it first fell, and will almost always be impossible to find without a retrieving dog. Not only is it pointless to go shooting without being able to pick up what you shoot, it is also inhumane to fail to make every effort to find and despatch wounded game, and a gundog is by far the most practical way of ensuring that, so far as is possible, you bring everything you shoot safely to hand.

But, of course, a dog is far more than a mere practical tool. It is a companion that will share with you the triumphs and disappointments of your shooting expeditions, a partner that will bring a new dimension to your rambles through fields and hedgerows, an indispensable member of the team. A dog will add to the excitement and sense of expectation as it eagerly greets you on a shooting morning, and in the evening when guns are cleaned and put away, it will join you as you relax and re-live the day's happenings.

Gundog roles

As we have seen, there are three basic tasks that gundogs fulfil: finding game, flushing it, and retrieving it after it is shot. These tasks create a number of convenient groups within which the gundog breeds can be classified. By far the most commonly encountered gundog breeds in the shooting field today are the spaniel and retriever breeds, which are used for a wide variety of rough shooting, game shooting and wildfowling activities. Pointers and setters are to be seen mostly on the grouse moors, while the continental hunt-point-retrieve breeds are undergoing a remarkable rise in popularity and are increasingly finding favour, especially amongst rough shooters.

Dogs for finding and flushing game

The job of the spaniel is to hunt game from dense undergrowth and to flush it over the Guns. Spaniels are therefore lively and energetic dogs that hunt busily through the thickest cover. Their long, tough coats

A team of English springer spaniels sweeps up after the end of a drive.

offer surprisingly good protection against rough thorns and brambles, but the tails of working dogs are normally docked to prevent the ends from becoming sore and damaged while they are hunting.

English springer spaniel

By far the most popular spaniel in the shooting field today is the English springer spaniel, bred to flush or 'spring' a wide variety of game. It is the ancestor of most of the spaniel breeds, and its willing, active temperament and great versatility make it the perfect companion

The English springer spaniel is a popular gamekeeper's dog.

for the rough shooter. The English springer was bred originally to hunt and flush, and is at its very best in the beating line, nose down and busily searching for game. However, it can also make a first class retrieving dog, and in practice the rough shooter's spaniel is normally a dual-purpose animal that hunts out game and then retrieves when it is called upon to do so. There are many excellent blood lines available, so if you are looking for an English springer puppy, it will not be difficult to find a good working litter. English springers stand up to 50cm in height, and have brown and white or black and white coats, often with a white tip to the tail, which helps the handler to see where his dog is working in dark, dense woodland.

Cocker spaniel

The smaller Cocker spaniel originated in the early 1800s in Wales and southwest England, where it was used to hunt the woodcock. Cockers are busy little dogs, though not so powerful as the English springer. Like them, however, they have a long, weather-resistant coat and very good scenting abilities. Standing at around 40cm in height, the cocker has found increased popularity in recent years, especially on the grouse moor. Cockers are also much-loved companion dogs, and because most of those kept as pets or for the show ring do not work in the shooting field, there has developed over the years a distinct difference between the working and the show strains of this breed. To their credit, some show breeders have done their best to ensure that their dogs

Above: The versatile English springer spaniel can make a first class retriever.

Left: Cocker spaniel at work on a grouse moor.

Top: Welsh springer spaniel.

Above: Sussex spaniel.

retain the ability to hunt game, but if you are choosing a cocker for shooting, then it is sensible to select a puppy from proven working parents.

Welsh springer spaniel

Originating as early as the 1500s, the Welsh springer spaniel probably shares a common ancestry with the English springer, but is rather smaller and has a more finely shaped head. Its coat, which is long, straight and silky, is white with rich chestnut red markings. Welsh springers have a friendly temperament, but are less busy and energetic than the English springer, as well as being harder to train. They are also considerably more rarely seen in the shooting field.

The Sussex spaniel, the Field spaniel and the Clumber spaniel are breeds that are not often seen out shooting. However, each of these minor breeds has its small band of enthusiasts who breed, train and use them for their traditional shooting role.

Sussex spaniel

The Sussex spaniel is an old breed, long and low in build, and with a rich liver-coloured coat. It is slow in temperament and unlike other spaniels, may 'give tongue' when in pursuit of game.

Field spaniel

The Field spaniel originated through the interbreeding of the springer and Sussex. Standing at around 45cm, it is relatively short in the leg and long in the body. The Field spaniel was originally very dark in colour but today has a flat, silky coat in rich shades of brown. Though relatively popular after the last war, the Field spaniel is rarely seen out shooting today.

Clumber spaniel

Bred by the 2nd Duke of Newcastle in the late 1700s at his Clumber Park estate in Nottinghamshire, the Clumber spaniel comes originally from French stock. It is a large, bulky dog, with a massive, square head and deep jowls. White with lemon markings, the Clumber is a slow, patient and methodical worker, and although Clumbers may take a long time to mature, some dogs are very reliable workers with very good scenting abilities.

Retrieving dogs

It is the task of the retriever to find and bring game back after it is shot. Because their primary job does not involve dashing about, finding and

Above: Clumber spaniel.

Left: A partridge brought to hand by an experienced Golden retriever.

flushing unshot birds, the retriever breeds tend to be rather more sedate in temperament than the lively spaniels. That, however, does not make them any less loyal and dedicated workers. Most retriever breeds have an easygoing nature, which makes them ideal family dogs.

Labrador retriever

Without doubt the most popular of all the retrieving dogs is the Labrador retriever. Bred from stock originally introduced into Britain from North America, the Labrador is a compact dog standing 55–60cm high, with a smooth, dense, waterproof coat, a kind and intelligent face, a powerful chest and a characteristic otter-like tail. It has an excellent nose with which to hunt and find shot game, and a placid temperament, which makes it especially good as a family dog. Labradors are often the first choice of the game shooter who wants a dog that will sit quietly and patiently throughout a drive and then eagerly pick up birds afterwards, but although this is the traditional role of the breed, Labradors can be just as much at home when hunting

Ready for action!

out hedges and dense cover for the rough shooter. Their enthusiasm when working in water is legendary, and this, coupled with the thick coat that keeps a Labrador warm all day in the most severe weather, makes this breed the automatic choice of most wildfowlers. Labradors may be either black or yellow, which includes every hue from pale straw colour through golden yellow to a sandy russet. Occasionally dogs are coloured a uniform chocolate brown.

Golden retriever

Second in the popularity stakes amongst the retriever breeds is the Golden retriever. Similar in size to the Labrador, the Golden retriever has a longer coat, soft in texture and a rich golden yellow in colour. Formerly known as the Golden flat-coat, it was bred originally from

Above: The Labrador's dense coat makes it ideal for working in water.

Left: An eager team of Golden retrievers with their handler.

Flat-coated retriever stock. The breed is very docile and affectionate, and its temperament has ideally suited it to the dual purpose role of gundog and family pet. Golden retrievers are good and reliable workers, with good game-finding ability, though they perhaps lack the flair of the Labrador. They are, nevertheless, quick learners and relatively easy to train.

Flat-coated retriever

In the early 1900s, the Flat-coated retriever was probably the most frequently seen of all the retriever breeds in the shooting field, and was particularly popular amongst gamekeepers. It was not until after the First World War that the breed started to decline, whereupon it was eclipsed by the Labrador and Golden retriever. However, the Flatcoat still has its supporters, and indeed is now undergoing a revival in popularity. It has a longer, more aquiline head than either the Labrador or Golden retriever, and has a long, silky coat, which is normally black, though brown dogs do occur. The Flatcoat is rather slow to mature, and so great patience is required in training.

The Flat-coated retriever was formerly the most popular breed amongst gamekeepers.

Next amongst the retriever breeds we come to three dogs that are particularly noted for their distinctive waterproof coats. The Curly-coated retriever, the Chesapeake Bay retriever and the Irish water spaniel are all minor breeds in the retriever world, but they can occasionally be found out shooting, and probably have their strongest support amongst wildfowlers who value their abilities as water dogs.

Curly-coated retriever

The Curly-coated retriever is a big dog, standing between 65 and 70cm high, with a distinctive short, dark, tight curly coat covering its body. Its head is large and powerful, and the facial hair is short and smooth. The Curly-coated retriever is one of the oldest retriever breeds, and probably shares some ancestors in common with both the Labrador and the Poodle.

Chesapeake Bay retriever

Originating in the eastern USA, the Chesapeake Bay retriever is said to have been bred from two puppies rescued from a ship that ran aground off the coast of Maryland in 1807. Its brown coat, wavy rather than curly, is very dense and has an unusual oily texture, which makes it extremely water resistant. This attribute makes the Chesapeake Bay retriever particularly well adapted to working in cold, wet conditions. A strong swimmer, the breed is most popular amongst wildfowlers.

Irish water spaniel

Though sometimes classified with the spaniels, the Irish water spaniel is not a true spaniel at all. Coming from a long line of curly-coated water dogs, the present breed was established in Ireland in the 1850s by Mr Justice McCarthy. A big and extrovert dog, it is covered all over in curly ringlets of liver-coloured hair which is naturally oily and water-repellent. The tail, however, is smooth and tapers to a fine point. As their name implies, Irish water spaniels are most at home in rivers, fens and marshes – the wetter, the better. Though they are slow to develop and take several years to mature, experienced Irish water spaniels are hard to beat when there are ducks or geese to be retrieved.

Irish water spaniel.

Pointing dogs

The pointers and setters are old established breeds whose task it is to find game and indicate its whereabouts to the shooter. Before the days of large, organised shoots, when sportsmen using muzzle-loading guns hunted game alone or in the company of one or two other shooters, shooting was a more leisurely activity than it sometimes is today. The need was for dogs that could 'quarter' or range back and forth across a grouse moor or the stubble fields of a partridge manor and, having located a covey of birds, ensure that they stayed put where they were until the shooters arrived.

Pointing dogs, or 'bird dogs' as they are often called in America, are therefore bred and trained to find game by means of its body scent. When working into the wind, so that the scent is blowing from the hidden game towards the dog, a good pointer or setter can detect birds or animals that are several metres away. It then stops and 'points' towards the game, characteristically thrusting its muzzle forwards, raising a foreleg and levelling its tail, signalling to the Guns to get into position for a shot. The dog should then remain perfectly still until instructed by its handler to flush the game.

German shorthaired pointers are amongst the most active of the HPR breeds.

English pointer

The English pointer is the breed most often associated with the pointing dogs. It is a fine, elegant animal, smooth coated and strong boned, and stands up to 70cm tall. English pointers are fast and active, often having to cover many miles of country as they range back and forth in front of the Guns. However, their scenting powers are extraordinarily well developed, and the deep muzzle and square cut jowl lends the head an almost regal air. The neck is long and strong, built to carry that all-important nose close to the ground as its owner travels at speed across the heather in search of game. English pointers may be black and white or red and white, with the coloured markings often set against a mottled background.

Below: English pointer on point at grouse.

Bottom: English setters at work.

English setter

The setters are slightly smaller and more lightly built than the English pointer, with heads that are rather less square cut about the muzzle, though no less aristocratic in appearance. Most obvious, however, is the fact that all the setter breeds are long coated, with fine, silky hair and well-feathered tails. The English setter was developed in the 1820s by Mr Edward Laverack, and for a while it was known as the Laverack setter. It is predominantly white in colour, but mottled with grey or brown.

Gordon setter

Gordon setters, on the other hand are black and tan in colour, and are the only setter to have been developed in Scotland, where they were bred originally by the Dukes of Gordon. A workmanlike dog, the Gordon setter is renowned for its stamina and perseverance. Though not as fast as the other setters, the Gordon is said to be particularly steady when on point.

Irish setter

The Irish setter's ancestry is unknown, but is most likely traced back to the spaniels, as the old Irish name of Red spaniel indicates. In colour, Irish setters may be anything from a golden chestnut to a deep mahogany red, while there are several working strains of dogs that are red and white in colour. The breed is noted for its keenness and endurance, though it is sometimes inclined to be headstrong and wilful. These days, the Irish setter is more likely to be seen on the show bench than in the shooting field.

Irish setter.

Gundogs that hunt, point and retrieve

There is one more category of gundogs to consider. These are the multi-purpose or Hunt, Point and Retrieve breeds – a description usually abbreviated to 'HPRs'. Originating in continental Europe, the HPRs are versatile dogs, designed to find and point game, to flush it on command and then to retrieve it afterwards. At their best when working for just one or two shooters, they can make ideal all-purpose hunting dogs for the rough shooter who is prepared to put in the considerable time and effort needed for training.

Ranging out in front of the Guns and running at speed through a field of roots or a wood, or along a hedgerow, the HPR will, like the pointing breeds, detect the presence of game by its air scent. Ideally, it should then point the bird or animal, allowing the shooter to get into position before the dog is sent in to flush. Remaining steady as the shot is fired, the dog should then retrieve on command.

It is fair to say that the average HPR will rarely carry out the individual hunting, pointing or retrieving tasks as well as the specialist spaniels, pointers and retrieving dogs, and there are several inherent vices that need careful watching, such as a tendency in some breeds towards hard mouth – the damaging of retrieved game by crushing it between the jaws. In addition, the HPRs tend to be rather more individualistic and slow to mature than the more conventional gundog breeds. Nevertheless, a good HPR is a joy to shoot over, as many more shooters are starting to discover. Almost unknown in Britain before the 1950s, when they were 'discovered' by shooters serving in the British forces stationed in Germany, these multipurpose dogs are now starting to receive the recognition they deserve amongst gundog enthusiasts in this country.

A German shorthaired pointer on point at grouse. The dog is wearing a GPS device to allow it to be tracked by its handler.

German shorthaired pointer

Some of the most popular HPR breeds were developed in Germany in the mid 1800s, and of these the German shorthaired pointer, or GSP, is the best known. It is a cross between the old German pointing dogs, the bloodhound and the English pointer, and is smooth coated and mottled with a liver and white or black and white colouring. The GSP is an intelligent and very active dog that needs plenty of exercise. It is a favourite amongst falconers and is used by some woodland stalkers for tracking shot deer.

German wirehaired pointer

Another mix of continental breeds, including the rough coated Griffon hound and the German Shepherd Dog has produced the German wirehaired pointer, or GWP. Very popular both in Germany and Scandinavia, the GWP is relatively new to Britain. It is of a similar build to its short-haired cousin, but has a rough, wiry protective coat flecked with liver and white, and a distinct 'beard' underneath its muzzle.

Weimaraner

The Weimaraner is one of the oldest German pointing dogs, and dates at least from the mid 1600s. It is sleek, muscular and an unusual grey in colour. Weimaraners, which originated from the Weimar area of Germany, have good noses and are obedient and friendly. Though the majority of dogs are smooth coated, a long-haired variant of the breed does exist.

Top: German wirehaired pointer.

Bottom: Weimaraner.

Large Munsterlander

Amongst the German HPRs the Large Munsterlander is the least commonly encountered in Britain, though it is a beautiful dog to look at, with a setter-like head and a silky, long-haired coat in black and white, often with attractive mottling on the legs. The tail is well feathered.

Vizsla

From Hungary comes the Vizsla, a smaller dog, though no less active in temperament than the GSP. Its smooth coat is golden russet in colour, and the Vizsla's ancestors include the ancient Transylvanian hound and the Turkish yellow dog.

Brittany

French crosses between local spaniel breeds and the English setter produced the Brittany, sometimes still referred to as the Brittany spaniel. This little dog, standing 45 to 52cm high, has the busy temperament of its spaniel ancestors, and looks not unlike a long-legged spaniel. It has a long, soft coat marked with tan and white.

Top: Hungarian Vizsla.

Bottom: Brittany.

Spinone

Two Italian HPR breeds have recently been introduced to shooters in Britain. The Spinone is a very ancient breed, dating back to the 1200s, and related to the Griffon. Its long, wiry coat protects it when hunting in thick, thorny cover, but although the spinone has a good nose, it is somewhat lacking in drive and perseverance.

Bracco Italiano

Likewise, the Bracco Italiano takes life at a leisurely pace. A heavy-boned, smooth-coated dog, distinctively marked in red and white patches and flecks, it has a head that is strongly reminiscent of that of a bloodhound. Though loyal, it is a slow maturing dog with a tendency towards stubbornness.

working life becomes even more important, particularly so with retrievers. A working retriever will have to sit quietly beside its handler, mark a falling bird and then, on command, use its eyes and nose or follow hand signals to locate the dead game. Finally, it must bring back the retrieve undamaged and deliver it promptly to the handler. How easy it is for all these lessons to be undermined by innocent and playful games such as the throwing of sticks when the dog is out for a family walk. In a few careless moments it learns that there is no need to wait for the command to retrieve, but that it is much more fun to gallop to where the stick is going to fall and then try to catch it as it does so. Then, as it chews at the stick on the way back, it realises that there is additional excitement to be had from a tug-of-war or a game of tag while the stupid human tries to grab the stick from out of its mouth.

In this way, a potentially brilliant retriever is taught to run-in to shot, to avoid promptly delivering game to hand while at the same time developing a 'hard mouth', which will damage game that it is in future sent to retrieve. The lesson is simple: never throw sticks for gundog puppies to pick up.

Working gundogs quickly learn that the most important person in their life is their master – and they will do anything for him.

There is another lesson, however, which will be learned much more easily if it is turned into a game. Often, a puppy is wary of entering water, and there is no better way to overcome its natural caution than to have a jolly good romp with it in a shallow stream or pond, or even on the beach. Plenty of splashing and excitement soon makes it realise that water is really good fun and certainly nothing to be frightened of, and unlike practically every other aspect of gundog training, the introduction to water is a lesson in which the presence of an older dog is positively beneficial.

> Once the bond with its master is forged in the shooting field, a good, well-trained gundog of whatever breed will do anything it can to please.

As the dog ceases to be a new arrival and starts becoming a member of the family, then everyone can start to share in the tasks of feeding, exercising and grooming. Most dogs will revel in the attention that they get, but no gundog will fail to recognise that the most important person is its master, its pack leader, the one that provides its sport and its purpose in life.

THE MYSTERY OF SCENT

As every gundog owner will confirm, the ability of a dog to locate a quarry bird or animal varies from day to day, even from hour to hour. Although dogs' noses are many times more sensitive than our own, even their extraordinary scenting powers are controlled by factors such as temperature, moisture, wind, and ground conditions.

Scent will tend to be better when the ground temperature is low. A cold winter's day will be far better for the dogs than a mild and muggy one in early autumn, and very often scenting conditions will improve towards the end of a winter's afternoon as the temperature drops. Damp conditions are better than dry ones, as the beads of moisture on the vegetation seem to allow the scent to cling, making it easier for retrievers to hunt the line of a wounded bird. Too much moisture, on the other hand, is a disadvantage. Torrential rain will only wash out any scent that is present, making it much harder for dogs to work properly.

Wind is a very important factor for dogs that rely on body scent in order to locate game birds or animals. Spaniels, HPRs and pointing dogs should always be encouraged to work into the wind, so that the scent of the quarry is blown towards them. If the wind is strong, it makes the dogs' work very difficult, and they may very easily miss a bird that sits tight.

Different ground surfaces carry scent to varying degrees. Where retrievers need to recover lost birds from thick cover, scent may be good. But if they have to follow a line over bare ground such as a ploughed field, then the lack of vegetation for the scent to cling to can make their job more difficult.

CHAPTER 10

The support team

THE SUPPORT TEAM

ALTHOUGH it may sound rather odd to say so, you do not need to have a gun in order to go out shooting. In fact, there are many people who take part in a day's shooting other than the shooters, and many of them gain at least as much enjoyment and satisfaction from their contribution as do the Guns themselves. Among them are those who look after and manage the habitat in order to encourage a healthy population of game birds and animals and there are those who rear and release game and protect it from predators. Then there are assistants such as beaters, stops and pickers-up, all of whom have important jobs to do, jobs that can make all the difference between the success or failure of the day's sport. Overall, this army of support staff amounts to the equivalent of 35,000 full-time workers providing shooting sports opportunities in the UK.

The head keeper and his underkeeper are the key members of shooting's support team.

Some branches of shooting, of course, require little in the way of a supporting cast. Wildfowling and rough shooting are mostly solitary sports, without any of the complicated planning or organisation associated with driven game shooting. But even so, wildfowlers often spend many hours in the summer months improving the wetland habitat and there is generally a warm welcome given to anyone ready to help a wildfowling club with clearing vegetation or repairing bridges and access routes to the marsh, while there is always a need for volunteers to help with feeding flight ponds during the autumn and winter. Rough shooters also find that there is invariably plenty of work to do on the shoot throughout the year. They appreciate that the regular topping-up of game feeding points in the woods will help to ensure that there are birds about on shooting days, and many rough shooters even go so far as to release a few pheasants or partridges to augment the wild stock. However simple the rough shoot may be, there is generally something for willing hands to help with.

The gamekeeper

When it comes to the more organised forms of sport, however, the key figure amongst shooting's support team is the gamekeeper. At one time, almost every estate had a head gamekeeper and often a team of several underkeepers working under him. Today, there are probably only about 4,000 full-time professional gamekeepers in Britain. However, they are backed up by thousands more part-time and amateur keepers who combine looking after the shoot with another paid job. Together, this army of gamekeepers does an immense amount to maintain game stocks and to manage the countryside.

Gamekeepers and habitat management

Game birds and animals are no different to any other forms of wildlife in that they require suitable habitat in which to flourish. One of the first tasks of the gamekeeper is therefore to ensure that the woods or moors are managed in such a way as to provide exactly the habitat that is needed. If the shoot is one where no reared game is released, then habitat conservation is even more important, for without it there will be little, if anything, for the Guns to shoot at.

Very often, habitat management involves controlling the growth of vegetation. Pheasants, for example, are birds of the woodland edge, and do not like dark, gloomy forests. So the gamekeeper on a pheasant shoot may often have to spend time cutting 'rides' or keeping the vegetation cleared from open pathways through the woods. The birds also prefer a wood that has a warm layer of undergrowth on the woodland floor to one that is cold and draughty. Gamekeepers also like to see that any hedges around the outside of the wood are warm and windproof, to provide additional shelter for birds.

> Encouragement of a warm layer of undergrowth generally means letting more light through from the tree canopy by selective felling and the creation of open glades within the wood.

The gamekeeper who is responsible for managing wild partridges will pay special attention to the hedgerows and field edges where the birds like to nest. He will try to ensure that the hedge itself is properly managed with a broad, thick base to provide shelter, and that the grass alongside it is tall enough for partridges to nest in without being spotted by predators. Equally, he will want to see near to the nesting sites sufficient areas of short grass where the young chicks can dry themselves after heavy dew or rain. Without this the tiny birds may quickly chill and die.

On the grouse moor, habitat management is a fundamental task for the gamekeeper. It is not possible to rear and release grouse and therefore the only way of ensuring that they are plentiful is to create the right habitat for wild birds to breed and successfully bring up large numbers of young chicks. This is done by burning, or in some cases flail mowing, small strips or patches of heather in the early spring. After the moor has been burned, new heather shoots very quickly sprout again to form a succulent carpet of young growth that the birds can feed upon, and within a few years, the young heather will grow up to form a thick, protective canopy within which the birds can nest in security. When it has become old and straggly, the heather is burned once again. So heather management, when carried out in rotation, creates a diverse and varied habitat, with areas of young growth interspersed with older heather to create exactly the conditions which grouse need.

In addition to this, the grouse keeper will aim to control disease by putting down medicated grit that combats the parasitic worms that can infest grouse and cause them to lose condition and eventually die.

Gamekeepers and predator control

As well as a suitable habitat in which to live, game birds and animals need security and freedom from predation if they are to thrive and multiply. If the gamekeeper can ensure that the game population contains a shootable surplus, then it will be possible during the season for a harvest of game to be taken without endangering the long-term future of the species. However, if the surplus that the keeper is trying hard to encourage ends up in the stomachs of foxes, or if its nests are raided by crows and magpies, then no matter how hard he tries, there will be little for the Guns to see or shoot at when the shooting season comes round.

The most important ground predators of game are foxes, rats and stoats, while feral mink can do great damage to game and wildfowl that is near to water where the mink live. Gamekeepers control foxes by shooting them with a rifle, often at night with the assistance of a powerful lamp or, increasingly, with image-intensifying or thermal-imaging sights. They may also use snares set on runs that foxes regularly use. Snares are designed not to kill foxes but to catch and restrain them so that they may be humanely dispatched with a gun. Guidance and codes of practice on the correct setting and use of snares are available on the BASC website.

Small predators such as mink or rats are normally caught in tunnel traps. These consist of an approved spring trap such as a 'Fenn' trap, which is placed in a small, specially constructed tunnel. Inquisitive ground predators entering the tunnel are humanely killed. Cage traps are also extensively used for pest control. These are often baited with food, and animals entering them are caught alive and dispatched later by the gamekeeper. By law, all traps and snares must be inspected every day.

Winged predators such as the carrion crow and the magpie do very serious damage at nesting time by plundering the eggs of pheasants,

A Larsen trap: in the left-hand section is a captive decoy or 'call bird' which has attracted a magpie into the right-hand catching compartment.

partridges and very many other wild birds. They have to be controlled, and this is normally done either by shooting or with cage traps. A particularly popular and effective cage trap is the 'Larsen' trap, invented by a Danish gamekeeper. It consists of two compartments. Into one of these is placed a live decoy bird, and this entices target birds down to the other compartment, which is fitted with a spring-loaded trap door. Once caught, the trapped bird is removed and destroyed. Larsen traps can be very effective in controlling the spread of magpies and crows and thus safeguarding the nests and eggs of other wild birds.

Most poaching is carried out by organised groups or gangs. These gangs are usually involved not just in poaching but in other aspects of rural crime, such as theft of farm machinery, livestock, or diesel fuel.

A further form of predator that the gamekeeper has to guard against is the two-legged variety, the poacher. Today, the romantic image of the old village poacher taking 'one for the pot' is a thing of the past. Most poaching is carried out by organised groups or gangs, who may take large amounts of game. These gangs are usually involved not just in poaching but in other aspects of rural crime, such as theft of farm machinery, livestock, or diesel fuel. Deer poachers often use particularly cruel methods that do not quickly kill the animal, such as snares, crossbows or low-powered rifles, and as a result they cause great suffering. Other poachers use dogs to course and kill hares or deer, and if challenged by the farmer, landowner or gamekeeper they will often become violent. Thus, the gamekeeper is the eyes and ears of the countryside, and he generally has a close working relationship with the local police.

Rearing and releasing game

On a great many shoots, pheasants, partridges and sometimes ducks are reared and released, and where this takes place it is the gamekeeper's responsibility to manage the rearing and releasing programme. This will often entail a great deal of work and very long hours, especially at busy times of the year such as when eggs are hatching or when day-old chicks are received from the game farm, and when the young poults are first released into the woods.

Some gamekeepers carry out the entire incubation and rearing process on their employers' estates, and this means that they have to start with large numbers of game bird eggs. These can either be bought from a specialist game farm or collected from hens that have been caught up at the end of the shooting season and put, together with a number of cocks, into a large open laying pen. The eggs then have to be incubated. Traditionally, this was done by large numbers of broody hens, which acted as foster-mothers to the young game bird chicks. Nowadays, however, gamekeepers use an incubator that can accommodate a large number of eggs at one time and keep them at a constant temperature until it is time for them to hatch. The young chicks are then reared to the age of six or eight weeks, when they are introduced to the wild. If the estate does not wish to undertake the entire incubation and rearing process itself, the gamekeeper may obtain day-old game bird chicks or six week old poults from a game farm. When they are first released into the woods, pheasant poults are put into a release pen. This is a large, open-topped pen that is normally situated in a wood and which encloses natural cover such as trees and bushes, in order that the poults can learn to fend for themselves. The sides of the release pen are about 3 metres (10 foot) high, and are made of netting that can be let into the ground in order to prevent foxes from digging their way in. Sometimes, a low electric fence is placed around the outside of the pen for added protection against foxes. At strategic points around the pen there are 'pop holes' in the wire through which, in due course, the birds may come and go. Water and food, normally whole grain, are supplied every day by the gamekeeper, and as they gradually get accustomed to their new surroundings, the birds will be allowed out through the pop holes to explore the wood adjacent to the release pen. By the beginning of the shooting season, the pheasants will be fully developed, flying strongly and completely accustomed to life in the wild. At this stage the release pen will be permanently open and the birds will be able to come and go as they please, the gamekeeper keeping them in the woods only by means of regular feeding.

Partridges are normally released not in woods but in specially established game cover crops out in the fields, while mallard are released onto a suitable lake or pond. Like pheasants, both partridges

Below left: Topping up feeders is one of the gamekeeper's many daily tasks.

Below right: This gamekeeper's pickup has been fitted with a spinner to help with the task of scattering wheat on the feed ride.

and mallard require constant attention to prevent them from straying in search of food.

With habitat management, predator control and game rearing to keep him occupied, the gamekeeper is busy at all seasons of the year. Very often, he will be glad of some extra help, and one of the very best ways in which to learn about how a shoot works is to offer to spend a few hours assisting him with tasks such as building and repairing release pens or carrying food and water for the birds. If you are lucky, you will begin to learn about the rearing and management of game and the skill and the fieldcraft involved in such activities as trapping and predator control. More than that, you will soon start to appreciate and understand about the lives and habits of the other wild creatures which live on or around the shoot.

Other shoot assistants

One occasion upon which help is always needed is on a formal shooting day, when a range of assistants is required to ensure that everything goes smoothly. Beaters, stops, and pickers-up may all be needed, and even the non-shooter can help with these tasks, learning much in the process and getting a great deal of pleasure out of a day in the countryside.

Beaters

The beater's job is to drive game towards the Guns, and although the task may sound a simple one, there is, in fact, considerable skill involved in beating, which makes it an enjoyable and interesting job as well as an energetic one. Beaters work as a team, usually under the supervision of a gamekeeper, and if you are spending a day beating, then the first rule to remember is that any instructions that you are given must be followed exactly. If you stray out of line or decide to go to a different part of the wood from that to which you were sent, then you will upset the carefully laid plans for the drive. Generally, the instructions to the beaters will be given

> The beater's job is to drive game towards the Guns and put the birds over them one by one in a steady stream.

verbally, perhaps via a radio, or by a blast on a whistle. Make sure that you know what the signals mean, and if an instruction is given temporarily to halt a drive, then stop immediately and do not move forwards again until you are told to.

Do not try to rush through the cover, for if you do so then you will almost certainly pass over birds that are sitting tight, and furthermore you will make it difficult for the other beaters to keep in a straight line with you. Remember that it is your job to put the birds over the Guns one by one in a steady stream, not to force them over in a single mad rush. The reason for this is that if all the birds flush together, then instead of being able to shoot throughout the drive, the Guns will have only one or two opportunities to shoot as the cloud of birds flies over them. As a beater, you will therefore need to watch closely for birds moving in front of you. If you see several that look as though they are all about to flush at once, then stand still and tap steadily with your stick until they flush one by one or until they move forwards into the next patch of cover.

The keeper and his team of beaters. An essential part of the game shooting scene.

If you have a dog, then you really can get enormous fun from working it in the beating line. There is no doubt that the presence of a few good dogs, spaniels in particular, makes all the difference to the success of a drive. The dogs will find and push up game that you never knew was there, producing many more sporting birds for the Guns to shoot at. However, your dog must be well trained, and must not be allowed to rush ahead, chasing game and flushing it in a wild and uncontrolled manner. Carry a slip-lead with you – a gundog should not wear a conventional collar when it is working in case it should get caught by brambles or barbed wire – and if your dog is becoming over-excited, then put the slip-lead on it and walk with your dog at heel. Never take a dog out beating without first checking with the gamekeeper that you may do so.

A dog is very useful for getting into those really tough pieces of cover that you will often find in the middle of a wood. However, if you do not have a dog with you, then you will have to try and bash through these places yourself, no matter how forbidding they may seem.

A good team of dogs is essential to the gamekeeper.

If you do not, then you can be quite sure that is where all the birds will be and that if you skirt round the outside, then you will miss them. Conversely, if you are working through a block of game cover crop, then make sure that someone walks around the outside of the cover crop, tapping with their stick as they go. If the outside of the cover is not guarded in this way, then the birds will quickly take advantage of the situation by running back around the outside of the cover crop, unseen by the beaters who are energetically bashing their way through the middle.

Another question to consider when beating is the extent to which you should use your voice. As a general rule, the wilder the birds, the less noise you should make. On a genuine wild bird shoot, the pheasants or partridges will run or flush the moment they hear the slightest noise, and all that is required is a steady tap, tap, tap with your stick as you move forwards. It is a real delight to watch an experienced team of beaters at work with wild game. Where reared birds are present, a little more verbal encouragement may be used, but even so, nobody wishes to hear shouting and yelling, and the best way of encouraging birds to move and flush in a controlled manner is to tap the bushes and undergrowth with your stick.

An experienced partridge keeper knows exactly when to use his flag in order to turn a covey of birds towards the Guns.

On a genuine wild bird shoot, the pheasants or partridges will run or flush the moment they hear the slightest noise.

When beating on a walked-up shoot, you may well be walking alongside the Guns. If so, and particularly if you have a dog with you, lend a hand by carrying any shot game back to the game cart or to the place where it is collected at the end of the drive.

Often, a number of beaters will be given flags, normally made from plastic fertiliser bags attached to sticks. These can be used to turn game birds such as partridges and grouse, and are particularly effective when game is being driven from open country, such as a field of roots or a grouse moor. Very often, a covey of birds that gets up will fly along the line of beaters rather than away from it, and if the birds are not quickly turned, then they will almost certainly escape out of the side of the drive. If you are given a flag, you may well be asked to walk in a strategic part of the beating line, such as on a flank or ridge over which the birds might be tempted to fly. Should you see any birds heading towards you, then wave your flag in an effort to turn them forwards and towards the Guns. Remember that flags are most effective when sparingly used. A well-timed wave at the critical moment will be far more effective at turning a fast-flying covey of partridges or grouse than a continual half-hearted flap.

If you are going out for a day's beating, then make sure that you dress sensibly, for you will almost certainly have to go through

Other local keepers will often help out on a shoot day.

Above left: There are plenty of jobs for everyone on a shoot day.

Above right: Beating is an enjoyable job for all ages.

thick, possibly wet cover. A thornproof, waterproof coat is best, and overtrousers or leggings will be an enormous help when walking through brambles or root crops such as sugar beet. Wellington boots are ideal for most situations. However, if you are invited to beat on a grouse moor on a hot August day, then you may well find that a pair of jeans and a T-shirt are all that you need. Even so, do remember to wear stout ankle boots and perhaps a pair of gaiters, for heather is very abrasive around your ankles.

The only thing you will need with which to go beating is a good stout stick.

Beating is open to both sexes and all ages, and most shoots are constantly on the lookout for good, reliable beaters, especially on weekdays. Of course, it helps if you already know the local gamekeeper, for it is his responsibility to recruit the beating team, but a few words with one of his regular beaters should soon give you that all-important introduction. And don't forget that if you have been beating regularly on a shoot throughout the winter, you may well find yourself a guest on the keeper's or beaters' day at the end of the season, when the gamekeeper has the chance of inviting for a day's shooting all those who have helped him during the course of the year.

Stops

A particularly important member of the beating team is the 'stop'. His or her job is to prevent game from leaking out of the side of the drive at a vulnerable point. A wood that forms the main part of a drive may, for example, have a ditch or hedgerow leading off it and connecting it with a neighbouring piece of cover. This escape route will be well known to all the game birds that live in the vicinity, and will be used as a natural corridor or pathway. When a line of beaters comes through the wood, the birds will naturally make a beeline for it. The result will be that instead of flushing and flying forwards over the Guns, they will leg it as quickly as possible along the ditch and disappear out of the drive. Unless, of course, they are prevented from doing so by a stop.

If you are asked to act as stop, then you should take up position before the start of the drive, standing at the point where the ditch or hedge leaves the main wood or cover which the beaters are working through, so blocking the exit route for any game. Remember that your objective should be to head the birds back into the wood rather than to put them up into the air. From the moment that the drive starts, you should tap quietly with your stick, watching closely for any birds that run towards you. Often, you will spot a steady procession of pheasants heading through the undergrowth in your direction, only to see them turn back into the wood the moment that they realise you are there.

Do not shout or make lots of noise: there is no need to do so. All that is required is that steady tapping, as this is without doubt the most effective way of ensuring that the birds go in the intended direction, over the Guns.

Loaders

On a big driven shoot where a lot of game is expected, or on a grouse drive where the action is expected to be very fast, the Guns will sometimes use a pair of shotguns and have a loader with them. When 'double gunning', the loader's task is to load one shotgun while the other is in use. When the Gun has taken a shot, he will pass the first gun to his loader who will exchange it for the second gun, which will have already been loaded. The procedure for passing shotguns between Gun and loader is very precise and will have been well rehearsed between the two individuals. This is the only situation in the shooting field in which one person may properly pass to another person a shotgun that is both loaded and closed.

Often, the shotguns will be a matched pair, built to identical specifications by the gunmaker so that the fit, weight and handling of the two guns is exactly the same. A pair of guns like this by a top maker represent the very summit of the gunmaker's craft.

Sometimes, a loader will assist a Gun who is using only a single shotgun by standing slightly behind and to the side of him and 'stuffing' cartridges into the empty chambers after a shot has been taken. This allows the Gun on a busy drive to concentrate on the birds in front of him rather than having to worry about reloading. Assistance like this can increase the rate of fire considerably during a rapid flush of game.

Double gunning on a partridge drive. The Gun takes a shot as the loader prepares to pass him the second gun.

Another occasion on which a loader might stand with a Gun is where a less experienced shooter requires guidance and support. In these circumstances the loader will be able to provide advice on which birds may be shot, maintain close supervision while shooting is in progress and ensure that only safe shots are taken.

Loaders will usually take charge of the shotguns after the drive, carrying them, looking after them and perhaps cleaning them at lunchtime or at the end of the day.

Pickers-up

Situated behind the Guns on a driven shoot are some very important members of the support team. Without the pickers-up and their dogs, a very large proportion of the shot game would probably never be recovered. While birds that fall in the open, near to the Guns, can usually be picked up with relative ease, those that drop several hundred yards behind the line, together with wounded birds that have sufficient strength to reach a distant piece of cover, must be carefully marked and then collected quickly by a dog.

> Without the pickers-up and their dogs, a very large proportion of the shot game would probably never be recovered.

The pickers-up and their dogs will watch each bird closely as it flies over the Guns. They will note those that are shot at and, even if these birds do not fall, watch for tell-tale signs that they have been hit by just one or two pellets. Perhaps the bird might flinch in mid air or perhaps a leg might drop as the shot is fired. If so, once the bird has landed, a dog will be sent to find it. Wounded birds such as these, together with those that drop well behind the line,

The picker-up and his team of retrievers stand well back from the Gun line to pick the shot birds.

will often be picked while the drive is in progress. Those that have fallen close to the Guns will be collected when it has finished, at which point the dogs will move in to hoover up the fallen game. Each picker-up will probably have with him or her a team of three or even four superbly trained dogs, so that the pick-up can be completed quickly and efficiently.

Sometimes, one or more of the Guns will have their own dog with them so that they can enjoy working it after the drive is over, to pick up their own birds. The picker-up should be aware of this and should check beforehand to see whether a Gun wishes to work his dog. If so, then the picker-up should take care to leave any birds that fall dead close to where the Gun is positioned, and concentrate instead on those which have fallen well behind the line.

It is considered a great honour to be invited to pick up at a big shoot.

It is considered a great honour to be invited to pick up at a big shoot, and only when you have one or more very well trained dogs that are absolutely steady and reliable, and probably several years of experience in the shooting field yourself, are you likely to be invited to go picking up. Nevertheless, if you get the chance, try to watch an experienced picker-up in action. To do so is to see gundog work at its best.

Good dogs are necessary when retrieving birds from dense crops or cover.

Left: One of the Guns directs a picker-up to a partridge that he has shot.

Below: The end of a successful drive. This keeper's smile says it all.

Dispatching game

There is a further task with which pickers-up, beaters, and indeed all who shoot, must be familiar, and that is the humane dispatch of wounded game. No shooter likes to wound the animals or birds he shoots, and a quick, clean kill must always be the ultimate objective whenever the trigger is pulled. However, an instant kill is an ideal that is not always achieved, and the gundogs will occasionally bring back a wounded bird that has to be killed right away. The best and most humane way of dispatching a bird is with a short weighted stick or 'priest', often with a head made of deer antler filled with lead. Holding the bird in one hand with its head and neck extended, you should smartly strike the back of the head with the priest. If this procedure is correctly carried out, then a single blow will be all that is required to kill a bird.

A rabbit or hare requires a different technique. Experienced vermin controllers are able, with a quick movement of the hand, to dislocate the neck vertebrae, and this is perhaps the quickest and most effective way of dispatching furred game. A very effective alternative, however, is to hold the rabbit or hare up by its hind legs with one hand, and then strike the back of its neck sharply and firmly with the side of the other hand, delivering a blow just behind the ears. This should break the neck instantly.

> All dispatching of game should be done quickly and discreetly, using methods that cause least damage to the carcass.

All dispatching of game should be done quickly and discreetly, using methods that cause least damage to the carcass. Do not, therefore, adopt the frequently used technique of holding a pheasant by the head and swinging its body round in a circle. If you are skilled, you may well break the neck quickly. If you are not, then you will more likely remove the head from the body. Finally, try to avoid dispatching wounded birds or animals in front of passers-by, where your actions might be misinterpreted or give offence.

Above: At the end of the drive, birds are brought to the game cart, checked and braced up.

Left: Game is brought quickly to the chiller where it is stored until collection by the game dealer.

CHAPTER 11
Shooting and the countryside

SHOOTING AND THE COUNTRYSIDE

ALTHOUGH the woods, moors and marshes of Britain may look natural enough, they are, in fact, part of a rural landscape that is almost entirely artificial. Since the time when successive waves of immigrant peoples – Neolithic, Bronze Age and Iron Age – first cleared the virgin forests in order to create farmland, the face of our countryside has been shaped by man. On a framework of hills, valleys, rivers and mountains supplied by Mother Nature, he has over ten thousand years crafted a covering, a minutely detailed mantle which, if studied with care and understanding, will reveal all manner of hidden secrets about its history and development.

The rural landscape may look natural, but it is almost entirely man's creation.

An old earthwork, a hedgerow, the curved boundary of an ancient woodland or the broad grass verges beside a country road all tell us something about the people who created the rural landscape, and the

economic and social pressures that made them dig, build, plant and hew. The activities that have done most to shape the British countryside are, not surprisingly, farming and forestry, for the production of food and timber have always occupied large tracts of land and continue to do so today. Close behind them, however, come field sports, and you do not have to look far to see the impact that the sport of hunting has made on the landscape. The reason that areas like the New Forest in Hampshire, Rockingham Forest in Northamptonshire, Wychwood Forest in Oxfordshire and dozens of other such areas remain wild and wooded is because long ago they were designated as hunting areas and their destruction or cultivation was prevented. Thanks to hunting, they remain ancient survivors in a modern landscape.

Some of the spirit of these forests and chases was later embodied in the estates of great landowners who created their own deer parks and, from the late 1700s onwards, planted many small woodlands in order to make the countryside more suitable for the increasingly popular sport of foxhunting. In the late 1800s, however, the rise of game shooting as an important economic activity and a central focus for the social structure of the countryside led to the complete redesigning of shooting estates and the planting of vast numbers of new woods, coverts and shelter belts, many of which still exist today. In a very real sense, shooting has helped shape the fabric of the countryside, and as we shall see, it still exerts a great influence over the management of the land, an influence that has helped to counterbalance some of the more extreme demands made by commercial farming.

Shooting and the farmed landscape

From around 1820 up to the Second World War, the British countryside changed very little. The landscape of small fields enclosed by hedges, banks or stone walls supported systems of mixed farming in which the raising of livestock and the growing of crops went hand in hand. However, wartime food shortages led to a complete reorganisation of agriculture, which modernised and mechanised throughout the 1950s and 1960s in an attempt to make Britain self sufficient in the food that her climate would allow her to produce. When in 1973 this country

More wheat but less wildlife habitat. Farm intensification has led to the loss of hedgerows, trees and woodlands.

joined the European Community and became part of the Common Agricultural Policy, the process of agricultural mechanisation and intensification gathered speed. Many miles of hedgerow were removed to create larger fields, old pastures were drained and turned over to cereal growing, and marginal land was brought under the plough. The changes to the countryside and its wildlife were very rapid indeed, and people now accept that many of these changes were damaging ones.

Landowners with traditional shooting estates, however, often resisted the financial pressures that encouraged more intensive farming. They knew that the loss of hedges and woodlands would damage or destroy the habitat for game birds. Even in places like East Anglia, where the changes in farming practice were at their most sweeping, farms and estates where the owner has an interest in shooting have retained more of their traditional landscape features such as hedgerows, woodlands and copses. Shooting has therefore helped to preserve the countryside.

In addition, shooting and game conservation also provide an important incentive for farmers and landowners to manage the land more sympathetically now and in the future. They see that if the habitat for game is improved, then they and their friends can get more enjoyment from shooting over their farms, or they can let the shooting rights in order to obtain extra income. In addition, they know that long-term improvements such as the creation of new woodlands and game coverts will improve the capital value of their farms. These more sympathetic approaches to countryside management which we see today have been strongly promoted by organisations like the GWCT.

Long-term improvements such as the creation of new woodlands and game coverts will improve the capital value of farms.

Farmers with an interest in shooting were among the first to create 'conservation headlands' – where the use of pesticide sprays is greatly restricted – or uncultivated grass margins around the edges of their cereal fields, where insect life may thrive. Some have created specific 'beetle banks' – narrow ridges or strips of tussocky grass where insect life can breed unmolested. Insects, in turn, provide food for young game bird chicks and many other bird species besides, contributing greatly to a more diverse bird population.

Improvement of farms for shooting has encouraged the planting of many thousands of hectares of new farm woodlands. These woodlands generally incorporate native tree species such as oak, chestnut, wild cherry and field maple. They are often carefully designed so as to take advantage of the natural topography of the land for shooting purposes and to create the best possible distribution of game cover on the farm. As they grow and mature in the years to come they will be

Above: This new farm woodland was planted by a shooting landowner to provide cover for game birds.

Left: Hedge laying in Gloucestershire. Field sports have provided the incentive to retain and manage traditional landscape features.

an important feature in the landscape, replacing at least some of the farmland trees that were lost in the two decades after 1960.

Those farmers with a particular interest in shooting have in many cases managed and conserved their hedges or planted new ones, because hedges are important for game. The banks on which they grow provide nesting sites for pheasants and, more especially, partridges. The hedges themselves provide shelter and form 'corridors' along which game may move around the farm. And on shooting days game is driven over hedges in order to provide more exciting sport. Likewise, farm ponds are often to be found on shooting estates, where they have been retained or newly created in order to provide habitat for species such as mallard.

Game conservationists have also had an important part to play in making the Government's farming policies more environmentally friendly. When 'set-aside' was first introduced in order to take farmland out of cereal production, farmers were forced by law to mow or cultivate their set-aside land in early summer – just at the very time that ground nesting birds were raising their young. The destruction of game birds and other wildlife by ploughs and mowing machines was immense, and the outcry against it was led by bodies such as the GWCT. Thanks in part to the strong pressure from shooting farmers, the set-aside rules were changed so as to avoid the need to mow or cultivate during the nesting season. When agri-environment schemes were developed in the late 1980s and early 1990s, research by GWCT helped with the formulation of schemes for the planting of wild bird seed mixtures that would provide food for seed eating birds right through the winter, and later with pollen and nectar mixes that would boost insect life, and especially pollinators such as honeybees.

Where shooting takes place, farmers are often more sympathetic towards the landscape and wildlife habitats.

The more environmentally sensitive farming practices that shooting has encouraged have not only boosted game birds. A whole host of other species of birds, animals, plants and insects has also benefited. Wild flowers like the

Far left: Agri-environment schemes have allowed many wild flowers to reappear on arable farmland.

Left: This wild flower meadow, managed as part of a shooting estate, provides a rich habitat for butterflies and other insect life.

Below: Research by the GWCT helped with the formulation of schemes for the planting of wild bird seed mixtures to provide food for seed eating birds through the winter.

poppy, ox-eye daisy and cornflower have returned in profusion to the conservation headlands and field margins, bringing with them a significant increase in the numbers of hedgerow butterflies. Mammals such as the brown hare are also enjoying the more diversified habitat which agri-environment schemes such as Countryside Stewardship have created. Farmers and landowners with an interest in shooting have promoted the greening of agriculture, and continue to provide a strong environmental input into Government thinking on countryside matters.

Woodlands

Woodlands and field sports have had a long association. As the Ice Age retreated and Britain finally became separated from the remainder of continental Europe, the country was cloaked in a single great forest, consisting of hazel, elm, oak, alder, small-leaved lime and a number of other species. Over the succeeding millennia, people gradually cleared large areas of forest to create land in which to farm and build their villages, but the 'wildwood' on the edge of the fields and settled areas remained a place where they could hunt game, and soon assumed further economic importance as a source of fuel, timber, building materials, grazing and animal food. Formal protection of woodlands was given as long ago as 1184, when the Assize of Woodstock preserved forests as Royal hunting grounds, and succeeding Norman and Plantagenet kings enlarged and expanded the network of Royal forests and private hunting reserves or 'chases'. Strict laws were enacted to protect the environment of the deer that roamed the forest, which successive monarchs and their nobles enjoyed hunting. These laws prevented the cutting down of trees and the grubbing up or 'assarting' of woodland to create new farmland. Forest wardens and foresters were made responsible for apprehending poachers and looking after the deer, and heavy penalties were exacted from offenders. Though the Royal forests contained large areas of open ground and were not by any means entirely wooded, the protection given to them in the Middle Ages ensured the survival of important wooded landscapes all over Britain.

Down the centuries, landowners have continued to plant and protect woodland for the purpose of sport, and in the nineteenth century the development of the great shooting estates saw the planting of extensive new woods as cover for pheasants. Despite the ravages of two World Wars, which saw much felling of valuable timber, many of these woods still exist today, and sportsmen continue to protect woods because of their value for game.

A recent survey showed that half a million hectares of woodland are managed for shooting in the UK, and that shooting farms and estates have planted 48,000 hectares of native trees.

They also continue to plant new woods. A recent survey showed that half a million hectares of woodland are managed for shooting in the UK, and that shooting farms and estates have planted 48,000 hectares of native trees. Research also has shown that the more large-scale the shooting activity, the more likely it is that woodland is managed for game.

Woods must be managed as well as being planted and protected, and shooting sportsmen have an excellent record in woodland

Woodland is an important part of a sporting farm or estate. Many woods remain in the countryside only because of their sporting value.

Well-managed woodlands are much more likely to be found where shooting takes place.

management. Pheasants are birds of the woodland edge, and prefer an open wooded habitat with plenty of glades where sunlight can reach the woodland floor. This has encouraged sporting landowners to revive the old practice of coppicing, a form of woodland management in which trees are cut down to ground level and then allowed to re-grow from the stumps or 'stools'. Traditionally, coppicing was carried out to provide timber for fuel, building, thatching, hurdlemaking and furniture making. Today, it is just as frequently undertaken to produce ideal habitat for game, and fifty-three per cent of shooting farms and estates maintain their woodlands by such means as coppicing or thinning.

Shoot management also involves creating and maintaining rides through the woods, on which standing Guns can be positioned on shooting days, and opening 'windows' in the woodland canopy in order that pheasants may be flushed out of the woods to present high, fast-flying sporting opportunities to the Guns below. Woodland management prescriptions are carefully detailed by organisations like the GWCT, in order that landowners and foresters may combine the best possible game shooting with their other woodland enterprises such as timber or fuelwood production.

Where woodlands are well looked after, a great range of wildlife species benefits. Sporting woodlands are home to several rare woodland butterflies such as the Duke of Burgundy fritillary, the white admiral and the purple emperor. Where coppicing is undertaken, wild flowers such as bluebells, primroses, violets and wood anemones thrive and bloom, as do many species of wild fungi. Woodland birds appreciate the diverse and well-managed habitat that shooting creates, and benefit from the protection to their eggs and young that is provided by the control by gamekeepers of winged predators like crows and magpies. Sporting woodlands are frequently noted for the variety of birdsong that can be heard in them during spring.

Finally, woodlands are home to the six species of deer that are found in Britain, and while their presence can complement the conservation of game and wildlife, they are not always welcome to the forester because of the damage they can do to the growing shoots and the bark of young trees. Sporting management will therefore often include the control of deer to acceptable levels. Properly regulated woodland stalking ensures a sustainable deer population and so prevents excessive damage to commercial timber or biodiversity, while perhaps

Shooting is important to the economy of the countryside, providing tens of thousands of jobs.

Right: A game dealer collects birds straight from the shoot.

Below left: Preparing wild game for the table. Few people outside the sport of shooting can hope to enjoy the satisfaction of eating what they themselves have harvested from the countryside.

Below right: There has been an explosion of interest in game among Britain's celebrity and TV chefs.

yielding a valuable extra income to the woodland owner in the form of venison or fees from client stalkers.

Wetlands

Wetlands are some of the most threatened of Britain's semi-natural habitats. For thousands of years, people have prized level sites along the flood plains of rivers or close to the edge of tidal estuaries in order to build their villages, towns, cities and ports, while the rich, deep alluvial soils of our river valleys have proved some of the most fertile for farming. As a result, only a tiny proportion of this country's once extensive marshes and wetlands remains in anything approaching its natural state. Yet, these places remain a vital habitat for hundreds of thousands of wildfowl and wading birds that migrate here in autumn and winter from the far north, and we therefore have an international responsibility to conserve and protect them.

Wetlands are a vital habitat for migratory birds.

These flooded washes are managed by wildfowlers as an internationally important site for breeding and over-wintering wildfowl and waders.

Bird conservation bodies have done a great deal by buying and managing important reserve areas, but wildfowlers, too, have been a major force for wetland conservation. Since 1908, when the Wildfowlers' Association of Great Britain and Ireland (WAGBI) was formed, wildfowlers have recognised that unless wetlands are protected, ducks and geese will disappear and with them the sport of wildfowling. The principles of habitat conservation are today embodied in WAGBI's successor, BASC, and around the country its 220 affiliated wildfowling clubs manage 105,000 hectares of marsh and wetland, over seventy per cent of which is officially designated as Sites of Special Scientific Interest because of its very high nature conservation value.

Wildfowlers undertake practical conservation activities, such as wardening sites, creating and maintaining access routes across marshes, clearing litter, tree planting, pond and water level management, cutting and management of vegetation and pest control. Very often, these activities are undertaken on behalf of voluntary conservation bodies such as county wildlife trusts, or the Government's own nature conservation agencies. Wildfowlers also help look after nature reserves situated within the sites where they shoot by providing manpower in the form of voluntary wardens.

Wildfowlers undertake practical conservation activities, such as wardening sites, creating and maintaining access routes across marshes, clearing litter, tree planting, pond and water level management, cutting and management of vegetation and pest control.

Many landowners with an interest in wildfowling own important wetland sites, and wildfowling clubs are increasingly buying other similar sites as they come up for sale. A valuable source of funds for land purchase is the BASC's Wildlife Habitat

Trust, which raises money for conservation from within the shooting community. Thus, very large areas of wetland, both around the coast and inland, are under the direct control of shooting owners who manage them in accordance with the best principles of conservation.

Because wildfowlers have a vested interest in the conservation of wildfowl habitats, they are also among the first to protest against plans to develop or destroy valuable wetland sites. Frequently, these plans are put forward by commerce or industry, and wildfowlers have contributed to successful campaigns against the building of destructive tidal barrages across our estuaries. They also, together with other traditional estuary users, add their voice to protests against further damaging developments like the building of marinas and industrial estates. In addition, wildfowlers monitor closely against pollution, and are often the first to alert the conservation authorities to accidents such as oil spills.

Their responsible work for conservation has earned wildfowlers the respect of many conservation bodies, and today they take their place alongside other interest groups whenever the planning or management of estuaries, coastal zones and other major wetland sites is discussed.

Moorlands

One of the most important types of landscape in northern Britain is moorland. The wide, open hills of the uplands, purple with heather in the summer and bleak and forbidding in winter, are highly valued for their scenic beauty and are also home to a unique range of wildlife. Indeed, some moorland species are found only in the British Isles. Heather moors, however, have found themselves under threat from over-grazing, afforestation, the spread of bracken and general neglect.

But, heather moors also have an important economic value, for they are home to that most prized of all game birds, the red grouse.

> Management of heather for grouse deliberately sets out to create a particularly rich and diverse habitat, and this, in turn, benefits a host of other species such as the golden plover, greenshank and merlin, all of which form part of the moorland wildlife community.

Nearly half a million hectares of moorland is used for grouse shooting, representing a third of the entire moorland area of Britain. Where grouse are plentiful, the financial rewards to the moorland owners are able to cover the high cost of continued traditional management of the heather by rotational burning. Over the last twenty-five years, grouse moor owners have regenerated and recovered 88,000 hectares of heather moor, 23,000 of them in the last decade.

Gamekeepers, as we have seen, burn or mow the heather in order to create a patchwork of different-aged growth, which enables a pair of grouse to rear a large brood of healthy chicks in a relatively small breeding territory. This is why a well managed moor supports the highest concentration of grouse. Management of heather for grouse deliberately sets out to create a particularly rich and diverse habitat, and this, in turn, benefits a host of other species such as the golden plover, greenshank and merlin, all of which form part of the moorland wildlife community. Some ninety-six per cent of the increasingly rare black grouse population is confined to the fringes of moors managed for red grouse, benefiting from predator control by grouse keepers. Thus a valuable conservation asset is maintained and managed, thanks to shooting. The management of grouse moors is also vital in preserving the carbon locked up in the underlying peat soils, but carbon sequestration can only be maintained while the peat remains wet.

Moorland management for grouse shooting produces a varied patchwork of habitats that are rich in wildlife.

Moor owners have plugged over 4,000km (2,485 miles) of moorland drainage ditches, thereby helping to re-wet peat bogs, and they are working to re-vegetate bare and eroding areas of peat. This mitigates climate change and, because grouse moors often act as a catchment for drinking water supplies, it also helps improve water quality.

Throughout the moorlands of Scotland and northern England, grouse shooting therefore has a fundamental role in preserving a unique landscape, wildlife and environmental resource, a fact that is well recognised by many of the conservation organisations and agencies. They appreciate that it would simply not be possible for the Government alone to continue paying the costs of moorland management, and that it is often only grouse shooting which is saving these important landscapes from destruction. In the case of the heather moor, shooting may be nothing less than a lifeline upon which the survival of the habitat depends.

Shooting and conservation

Shooting and nature conservation are inextricably linked; indeed, they are dependant upon one another. It is self evident that unless quarry populations are conserved by the activities of people like gamekeepers and other land managers, shooting could not possibly exist. What

Never has more of Britain's countryside been shot over.

is less obvious, however, is that a great deal of nature conservation actually depends on shooting. Only a tiny proportion – around two per cent – of the land surface of Britain is covered by nature reserves, in which official policy and resources work towards the survival of wild species. Shooting, on the other hand, plays a part in the management of 14 million hectares, around two-thirds of the area of rural land in the UK. Whether it be on moorland or marsh, farmland or forest, shooting management improves the habitat for an enormous variety of plant and animal species, far beyond the relatively small number of game birds and mammals for which sportsmen have a direct and primary concern. The income that shooting provides, and the interest in conservation that it sustains amongst land managers creates a very real incentive for the protection and care of the countryside.

Without the income and the enthusiasm for voluntary conservation that shooting generates, it is hard to see how Government-funded conservation, provided at the taxpayer's expense, could cope. Without shooting, the countryside would most certainly be the poorer.

Far left: These members of a DIY shoot are building a new release pen. There is always something to do on the shoot that will get you out into the countryside, even during the close season.

Below: A shoot supper at the local pub. Shooting remains at the heart of the rural community.

APPENDIX

The Shooting Organisations

The British Association for Shooting and Conservation

Marford Mill
Rossett
Wrexham
LL12 0HL
Tel: 01244 573000
Email: enq@basc.org.uk
Website: www.basc.org.uk

Countryside Alliance

1 Spring Mews
Tinworth Street
London
SE11 5AN
Tel: 020 7840 9200
Email: info@countryside-alliance.org
Website: www.countryside-alliance.org

Game & Wildlife Conservation Trust

Burgate Manor
Fordingbridge
Hampshire
SP6 1EF
Tel: 01425 652381
Email: info@gwct.org.uk
Website: www.gwct.org.uk

INDEX